Post Tribulation Rapture

*A Biblical Study
of the Return of
Christ*

Roy W. Anderberg

Post Tribulation Rapture: A Biblical Study of the Return of Christ

Comments to author: goldstriker123@yahoo.com

Published by Wheatmark®
610 East Delano Street, Suite 104, Tucson, Arizona 85705 U.S.A.
(888) 934-0888 ext. 3
www.wheatmark.com

ISBN: 978-1-58736-018-3
LCCN: 2007943269

Preface

This brief study is for the lay student of the Word, and it is assumed that the reader has a fundamental understanding of the Bible and has heard or read about the return of Jesus Christ. All of the bold type are direct quotations from the Authorized Version of the Bible with their corresponding references. The content of the study may not make much sense to the unsaved person, which indeed maintains what the Apostle Paul said to the believers, *"¹⁴But the natural man* (unsaved) *receiveth not the things of the Spirit of God: for they are foolishness unto him: neither can he know them, because they are spiritually discerned"* (I Cor. 2:14). The only prayer that God will hear from the unsaved, is the prayer of repentance, and the acknowledgement that only Christ can forgive sin and grant salvation.

It is also the position of this author that the return of Christ is pre-millennial, that is, a belief that Christ will return for the purpose of rescuing Israel, and to set up a literal 1000 year kingdom; and if you are amillennial (see glossary) in viewing the return of Christ, this study, most likely, will not generate much excitement (see chart #1 for the various millennial views). This is a treatise that attempts to define prophetic terms and phrases, and then tries to place them in relation to each other, while endeavoring to place them all in relation to the 70th week of Daniel. I fully realize that there are many detailed variations by different authors of the same position. The four basic positions are: Jesus comes at the beginning of the week (pre-trib), He comes in the middle (mid-trib), He comes sometime in the 2nd half (pre-wrath) or He comes at the close of the week (post-trib). Within each position, there can be lots of variations, and indeed, there are!

I have also constructed a reasonably objective glossary/dictionary for a clearer definition and review of the many terms used in this discourse. The various terms are defined from a pre-millennial viewpoint, while also considering the various rapture positions and the deviations within each position. In addition to the glossary, there are 14 detailed charts that have been placed in the middle of the book to assist in the interpretation and the visualization of the various positions and terms.

As you study, I think that you will find that there is nothing more refreshing and rewarding than to mine the scriptures and find nugget after nugget of pure gold that has been tried in the fiery furnace of truth and stood the test of time.

I pray that this short discourse will stimulate the minds of other fellow Christians and after all is said and done, God will receive His worthy glory. I pray also that this will be a source of light, much like a beacon is for a ship in a stormy sea. The journey for the weary pilgrim may be closer to the end then many of us realize; so let us keep on 'keeping on' until He returns or calls us home to glory. So, with that in mind, let us carefully examine the subject of the return of Christ and some of the various details surrounding that event.

In His service, Roy W. Anderberg

Table of Contents

Table of Charts

The Return of Jesus Christ

A Biblical Study

We find that there are different views as to when the coming (Grk. - parousia) of Jesus Christ occurs in relation to the 70th week of Daniel (which is the final 7 year period, of the 70 weeks of years, which ends with everlasting peace for Israel – described in Daniel 9:24-27). This study primarily evaluates three popular views with respect to the location of the parousia:

1) The "pre-tribulation" rapture theory, which is a theory that advances the idea that the 70th week of Daniel is all tribulation and the wrath of God. The position holds there are two comings of Christ: one at the beginning of the final 7 year period, and another at the end of the 7 year period. They see the entire week as the tribulation period, thus calling it the "7 year tribulation period" (charts #2, 4, 5, 7).

2) The second viewpoint under discussion is the "post-tribulation" doctrine which sees the first half of the 70th week as a pseudo time of peace in Israel, and that the coming of Christ is a single final event occurring at end of the 7 year

1

period. Advocates view the 2nd half of the week as the tribulation period (charts #2, 8).

3) The third position mentioned, is the "pre-wrath," which sees the coming of Christ sometime in the 2nd half of the week immediately following the "shortened" tribulation. Supporters of this theory see the 1st half of the week as a pseudo time of peace, but view the tribulation period as an unknown shortened length of time; however, they do not shorten the 2nd half of the week (charts #2, 6).

There are 14 detailed charts that have been placed in the middle of the book for reference, helping to illuminate the various positions and the placement of frequently used terms. The models have been constructed to reflect events based upon the most common interpretation of those positions, bearing in mind, that there are deviations within each position. Fundamentally, in connection with the rapture, you are either: post-week, pre-week, or pre-wrath, all to be considered shortly. There is, however, chart #3, which we all amazingly agree on. This should be one of the first charts that you look at if you are not familiar with the other models. It would be fair to say, that everything that is not on chart #3 is most likely debated.

It should be noted that the term "7 year tribulation period" has been incorrectly assigned to represent the entire 70th week of Daniel, causing considerable confusion in terminology. The problem that arises when we use the term "tribulation," is that everyone has a different idea as to its length and when it starts or ends; but if you reference the tribulation to the beginning of the week, the middle, the 2nd half, the end, etc., then all envision the same location. The term was assigned by the pre-tribulation adherents much like several other terms (e.g. 144,000 "witnesses" or "144,000 evangelists"). The term 70th week comes from Daniel 9:27 which says, *"And he* (Antichrist) *shall confirm the covenant with many for one week:* (7 years) *and in the midst of the week* (3-1/2 years later) *he shall cause the sacrifice and the oblation to cease..."* There is nothing in Gabriel's statement to Daniel that implies that the entire week is tribulation, but only that Antichrist causes the sacrifice and offerings to cease in the middle. The term *"great tribulation"* originates by the mouth of Jesus, which He says comes because of the abomination of desolation. Jesus declared, *"When ye therefore shall see the abomination of desolation...flee...For then shall be great tribulation."* (Mt. 24:15-22 – emphasis added). The tribulation period is 42 months which is the time that Antichrist and the false religious prophet have total control over the saints (Rev. 13:4, 11:2). This book will generally reference everything in relation to the 70th week, but for the sake of the familiarity of positions, I will frequently use, pre-trib, pre-wrath, mid-trib, and post-trib.

Whether the Church is around during Israel's great tribulation or not, could make a significant difference in the mental and physical preparedness of believers to face really tough times. It certainly would not be comforting to find out that we were not prepared for a time of intense tribulation because we were taught that we would never go through it – how discouraging that would be. In the evaluation of the three positions, it is assumed that the reader has a fundamental understanding of the Bible, and believes that Jesus is coming again: bodily, visibly and with great power, and that every believer and unbeliever will see Him. It is biblical truth and understanding that we seek, and not just the adherence to a position that we possibly have been taught many years ago and have never given the subject a real personal study. If you have thoroughly studied the different positions and understand the different aspects of them, and then decide to choose one based upon the best scripture possible, that's one thing; but clinging tenaciously to a viewpoint without knowing the other positions, or accepting a belief when faced with contrary scripture; that is another matter. We need to be honest in our studies of the scripture keeping in mind that we are all servants and children of Almighty God and are commanded to love one another. I certainly do not claim to be anything or anybody by way of importance; but I do know for sure the scholars don't have all the answers either. The lawyers, Pharisees, and the entire Sanhedrin all had it wrong in regard to who Jesus really was, so I will trust in the leading of the Holy Spirit (Prov. 16:3). The issue before us is certainly <u>not</u> one involving salvation, and timing of the rapture should <u>never</u> be a part of a Church, or mission boards doctrinal statement requiring one to choose between them before you can join in fellowship with other believers or to serve on a foreign field. The subject should not be divisive, but rather challenging and fun – remember, the angel who told of future things to Daniel said, *"...Go thy way, Daniel: for the words are closed up and <u>sealed till the time of the end.</u>* (Dan. 12:9). This statement implies that as we get closer to the end of *"last days,"* that the Holy Spirit will reveal more truth. The absolute truth is; He's coming again! Perhaps we should all re-evaluate our positions from time to time in light of the angels statement to Daniel.

Most leading proponents of the "pre-tribulation" rapture theory view the entire seven years of the 70th week as the *"wrath"* of God. It is maintained that the Church cannot be present or have any part in that week because it is strictly

Jewish in nature. As a result of that thinking, they remove the Church prior to the beginning of the week, creating a number of difficulties when viewing several other scriptures and events. The idea of a "crown without a cross" (removal of the Church before the 70th week begins) is being scripturally challenged more and more as the day of His coming approaches. This author held to a "pre-trib" position for over 30 years, but when someone challenged my belief, I began to study the subject with great intensity. I found that there were many conflicting passages that "shot down" my well rehearsed model. It was a difficult switch because of what I had been taught in the 1950's and on into the 1970's. So, I will give you my thoughts on the different aspects of His coming and appearing.

It is my intent in this brief study, to demonstrate, beyond a reasonable biblical doubt, the following:

1. That the coming (parousia) of Christ is the same event as His appearing and revelation, and it is a single one time event.

2. That the parousia occurs at the end of the week or shortly thereafter.

3. That the cosmic events associated with the parousia in Matthew 24 are the same ones that Isaiah, Joel, Peter, Jesus, John and Paul prophesied or wrote about.

4. That the day of the Lord is connected directly with the parousia and happens immediately after the rapture.

5. That the day of the Lord is at the end of the week and Christians will not be surprised as it approaches.

6. That the 6th seal initiates the same cosmic events and intro-

5

duces the wrath of God upon unbelievers. The believers are not the subjects of God's wrath.

7. That the end of the world (age), and the time of harvest occur simultaneously at the end of the week or shortly thereafter.

8. That the last day, and the last trump also occur simultaneously at the end of the week or shortly thereafter.

9. That the two witnesses are killed and resurrected at the end of the 70th week.

10. That the Holy Spirit remains with the saints during the entire 70th week.

11. That the "restrainer" in II Thessalonians, chapter 2, is not the Holy Spirit but Michael (one of the chief princes and defender of Israel) He would be a better contender for the position.

12. That the rapture is neither silent nor secret, and is the same coming (parousia) that Jesus talks about in Matthew 24, transpiring at the end of the week or shortly thereafter.

13. That the rewards for believers are not dispersed anytime during the week, but rather at the appearing of Christ and the kingdom setup.

In the above 13 declarations, I have used the term, "or shortly thereafter." I say that because there is a lot of activity and events occurring at the end of the week, and beyond. There are two specific time periods totaling 75 extra days after the end of the great tribulation. Daniel mentions the 1290 days, *"And from the time that the daily sacrifice shall be taken away, and the abomination that maketh desolate set up, there shall be a thousand two hundred and ninety days"* (1290 days

- Dan. 12:11). Concerning the 1335th day, he declares, *"Blessed is he that waiteth and cometh to the thousand three hundred and five and thirty days"* (Dan. 12:12 – this could be the "actual" start of the kingdom). Many events will be taking place within the 75 extra days that Daniel talks about (Dan. 12:9-13), and there are other events which occur after the 75 days which the Bible records, but the sequence of them just hasn't been revealed clearly enough to be dogmatic. So any discussion on those days will be pure speculation at best, and that is what this study tries to minimize, so we will not go there.

In Mt. 24:29, Jesus Christ has placed His parousia (coming) immediately after the great tribulation, and after a number of well defined cosmic events (Mt. 24:29-30). The parousia is presented in scripture as a singular event and is referred to as *"His coming," "the coming, "Thy coming,"* etc. There is no apparent biblical justification for two parousia's, nor can there be two phases! Paul said, *"So Christ was once offered to bear the sins of many; and unto them that look for him shall He appear the second time without sin unto salvation"* (Heb 9:28). In this verse Paul communicates a single, "one time" coming of Christ; there is no description of a "u-turn" back up to Heaven and then another coming several years later. To establish another coming, or another stage of the parousia prior to the tribulation, there must be biblical support at least as clear as the teaching of the post-trib singular parousia that Jesus and Paul taught. By establishing two parousia's, or two phases of the parousia, the timing of several major events are forced into an awkward position. This happens because certain events belong together with the rapture like salt and pepper go together, or snowballs in Alaska, or like palm trees in Miami. One of those major events is called the *"day of the Lord"* and it is

7

agreed on by most Bible commentators that the parousia tags along directly with the rapture. I am not suggesting that the day of the Lord and the rapture are interchangeable, but their arrival and relationship are intimately, and imminently close together – first our bodily resurrection and then God's wrath upon unbelievers.

Charts #4 and #5 are the typical pre-tribulational view of the various end-time events, in relation to the 70th week. Although pre-trib adherents may not place all of them there voluntarily, they must be there if the rapture is there. As an example, if you place the resurrection at the beginning, then the *"last day"* must be there whether you would like it to be there or not; and that is because Jesus said that He would raise us at the *"last day."* So, we will discuss events 1-10 (chart #4, to the left of the arrows) in the order shown. After our study, it will be demonstrated that many of these 10 events cannot occur at the beginning of the week. This model (chart #4), is the result of placing the rapture at the start of the week, or sometime before. The pre-trib model is in contrast to the post-trib chart #8 and the pre-wrath chart #6.

Before discussing the *"day of the Lord,"* a comment is in order. There are a few students of the Word who separate the phrase *"day of the Lord"* from the rapture by as many as 7 years to accommodate the problem of where the real placement of the day of the Lord should be; one of those is the popular Bible teacher, John MacAuthur. He places the *"day of the Lord,"* in what I view as the correct position (end of week), but places the rapture 7 years before. He states, *"And then, we come to chapter 6, (of Revelation) and from chapter 6 all the way through chapter 18, there is judgment, a time of great judgment. It unfolds in seal judgments and trumpet judgments and bowl judgments, and it ends*

8

with a holocaust of horror called the Day of the Lord, in which God's final fury is poured out" (tape GC-66-76). This is a significant deviation from most pre-trib commentators of which will be addressed later as we go. I have never personally talked to any pastor who believes that the *"day of Christ"* in II Thess. 2:2, is any different than the *"day of the Lord,"* or that there is a separation of 7 years between the events. The KJV and the NKJV are the only translations which use the phrase, *"day of Christ"* in the Thessalonians text – all others use *"day of the Lord,"* which, without doubt, are one and the same. For our discussion, we shall assume that the two phrases *"day of Christ"* and *"the day of the Lord"* are one and the same and occur immediately after the rapture and resurrection.

(1), (5) The Day of the Lord and the Cosmic Events

This phrase *"day of the Lord"* is mentioned 23 times in the Bible, most dealing with prophecy related to the end of the age. There are however, a few of those passages, that portray God's wrath as "soon to happen," (Babylonian captivity); but the same *"day of the Lord"* that was imminent to the captivity of Judah, would also be future to the 70th week, having a dual association. Sometimes it is difficult to discern which is which, but there are undoubtedly sufficient verses to establish the connection between the wrath of God upon Judah then, and the future fulfillment to us. There is controversy as to its length; for some suppose it is very long (1007 years), while others view it as a literal 24 hour day, while still others believe it to be several months or years. Most pre-trib (pre-week) enthusiasts see that day as including the entire 70th week and on through the millennial kingdom as shown in chart #9 (a view held by Dwight Pentecost in his book, *'Things to come'* and Scofield, in his Scofield Reference Bible). This particular viewpoint is held because of the phrase *"in that day,"* which is used with frequency in the Old Testament. However, it should be noted that the two terms, *"day of the Lord"* and *"in that day"* do not always relate to the same event and are <u>not</u> interchangeable on all occurrences, whereas the phrase, *"day of the Lord"* always has a negative judicial action involving God's wrath. There are times, however, when these two phrases appear to be linked, but *"in that day"* (millennium), is always precluded by the day of the Lord's wrath. Additionally, pre-tribulationalists view II Peter 3:10 as support for extending the *"day of the Lord"* beyond the week. But the passage in II Peter 3 is discussing the parousia of Christ (e.g. *"where is the promise of His coming?"*) in connection with the day of the Lord; Peter then declares that the *"day of the Lord"* will come as *"a thief in the night."* One might ask, "who would Jesus come as a thief in the night to after He has been reigning for 1000 years?" The idea of a restoration at the beginning of the 1000 years, or shortly thereafter, agrees with Isaiah 65 and 66, and also appeals to common sense. The horrific judgments themselves demand a complete restitution of all things at the beginning of the kingdom, otherwise that land could not *"blossom as a rose"* (Isa. 35:1). Also in Acts, 3:19-21, Peter reminds the Jews that Christ would completely restore the land when He returned.

The pre-tribbers also tack on an extension of 7 years because they believe the rapture and the day of the Lord both belong at the beginning of the week. The post-trib people place it at the end of the week because of: the cosmic events, the opening of the 6th seal, and the appearance of Elijah prior to that day. The pre-wrath view include the trumpets, vials, and Armageddon and factors in a "shortened tribulation" period, making it a couple of years or so in the 2ⁿᵈ half of the week (Marvin Rosenthal's view). Again, on chart #9, three different views of the length of the *"day of the Lord,"* and their starting location, are displayed. The starting point is absolutely crucial in determining where the rapture will be placed. In further discourse we will attempt to locate, scripturally, where that day starts; once that is established, then the rapture can be located with reasonable assurance of accuracy.

I think that it is important that the verses pertaining to the phrase and event, *"day of the Lord"* be listed and studied from both Testaments. The following verses should present a clearer picture; however, there are many other verses that allude to that day, but we will use only the ones that contain the direct phrase, *"day of the Lord."* They are as follows:

Isa. 2:12 "For the **day of the LORD** of hosts shall be upon every one that is proud and lofty, and upon every one that is lifted up; and he shall be brought low…"

Isa. 13:6-13 "Howl ye; for the **day of the LORD** *is* at hand; it shall come as a destruction from the Almighty. ⁷Therefore shall all hands be faint, and every man's heart shall melt: ⁸And they shall be afraid: pangs and sorrows shall take hold of them; they shall be in pain as a woman that travaileth: they shall be amazed one at another; their faces shall be as flames. ⁹Behold, the **day of the LORD** cometh, cruel both with wrath and fierce anger, to lay the land desolate: and he shall destroy the sinners thereof out of it. ¹⁰For the stars of heaven and the constellations thereof shall not give their light: the sun shall be darkened in his going forth, and the moon shall not cause her light to shine. ¹¹And I will punish the world for their evil, and the wicked for their iniquity; and I will cause the arrogancy of the proud to cease, and will lay low the haughtiness of the terrible. [12]I will make a man more precious than fine gold; even a man than the golden wedge of Ophir. [13]Therefore I will shake the heavens, and the earth shall remove out of her place, in the wrath of the LORD of hosts, and in the day of his fierce anger."

Ezek. 30: 3 "For the day is near, even the **day of the LORD** is near, a cloudy day; it shall be the time of the heathen."

Joel 1:15 "Alas for the day! for the **day of the LORD** is at hand, and as a destruction from the Almighty shall it come."

Joel 2:1-11 "For the **day of the LORD** cometh, for it is nigh at hand; [2]A day of darkness and of gloominess, a day of clouds and of thick darkness, as the morning spread upon the mountains: a great people and a strong; there hath not been ever the like, neither shall be any more after it, even to the years of many generations. [3]A fire devoureth before them; and behind them a flame burneth: the land is as the garden of Eden before them, and behind them a desolate wilderness; yea, and nothing shall escape them. [4]The appearance of them is as the appearance of horses; and as horsemen, so shall they run. [5]Like the noise of chariots on the tops of mountains shall they leap, like the noise of a flame of fire that devoureth the stubble, as a strong people set in battle array. [6]Before their face the people shall be much pained: all faces shall gather blackness. [7]They shall run like mighty men; they shall climb the wall like men of war; and they shall march every one on his ways, and they shall not break their ranks: [8]Neither shall one thrust another; they shall walk every one in his path: and when they fall upon the sword, they shall not be wounded. [9]They shall run to and fro in the city; they shall run upon the wall, they shall climb up upon the houses; they shall enter in at the windows like a thief. [10]The earth shall quake before them; the heavens shall tremble: the sun and the moon shall be dark, and the stars shall withdraw their shining: [11]And the LORD shall utter his voice before his army: for his camp is very great: for he is strong that executeth his word: for the **day of the LORD** is great and very terrible; and who can abide it?" (notice the last few words, "who can abide it" - same language as in Revelation. 6:17, and Malachi. 3:2 when speaking of God's wrath at the 6th seal).

Joel 2:31-32 "The sun shall be turned into darkness, and the moon into blood, before the great and the terrible **day of the LORD** come. [32]And it shall come to pass, that whosoever shall call on the name of the LORD shall be delivered: for in mount Zion and in Jerusalem shall be deliverance, as the LORD hath said, and in the remnant whom the LORD shall call."

Joel 3:12-17 "Let the heathen be wakened, and come up to the valley of Jehoshaphat: for there will I sit to judge all the heathen round about. [13]Put ye in the sickle, for the harvest is ripe: come, get you down; for the press is full, the vats overflow; for their wickedness is great. [14]Multitudes, multitudes in the valley of decision: for the _**day of the LORD**_ is near in the valley of decision. [15]The sun and the moon shall be darkened, and the stars shall withdraw their shining. [16]The LORD also shall roar out of Zion, and utter his voice from Jerusalem; and the heavens and the earth shall shake: but the LORD will be the hope of his people, and the strength of the children of Israel. [17]So shall ye know that I am the LORD your God dwelling in Zion, my holy mountain: then shall Jerusalem be holy, and there shall no strangers pass through her any more."

<u>Amos 5:18-20</u> "Woe unto you that desire the **day of the LORD!** to what end is it for you? the **day of the LORD** is darkness, and not light. [19]As if a man did flee from a lion, and a bear met him; or went into the house, and leaned his hand on the wall, and a serpent bit him. [20]Shall not the **day of the LORD** be darkness, and not light? even very dark, and no brightness in it?"

<u>Obadiah 1:15-16</u> "For the **day of the LORD** *is* near upon all the heathen: as thou hast done, it shall be done unto thee: thy reward shall return upon thine own head. [16]For as ye have drunk upon my holy mountain, so shall all the heathen drink continually, yea, they shall drink, and they shall swallow down, and they shall be as though they had not been."

<u>Zephaniah 1:7-9</u> "Hold thy peace at the presence of the Lord GOD: for the **day of the LORD** is at hand: for the LORD hath prepared a sacrifice, he hath bid his guests. [8]And it shall come to pass in the **day of the LORD'S** sacrifice, that I will punish the princes, and the king's children, and all such as are clothed with strange apparel. [9]In the <u>same day</u> also will I punish all those that leap on the threshold, which fill their masters' houses with violence and deceit."

<u>Zephaniah 1:14-18</u> "The great **day of the LORD** is near, it is near, and hasteth greatly, even the voice of the **day of the LORD**: the mighty man shall cry there bitterly. [15]That day is a <u>day of wrath</u>, a day of trouble and distress, a day of wasteness and desolation, a day of darkness and gloominess, a day of clouds and thick darkness, [16]A day of the trumpet and alarm against the fenced cities, and against the high towers. [17]And I will bring distress upon men, that they shall walk like blind men, because they have sinned against the LORD: and their

blood shall be poured out as dust, and their flesh as the dung. [18]Neither their silver nor their gold shall be able to deliver them in the **day of the LORD'S** wrath; but the whole land shall be devoured by the fire of his jealousy: for he shall make even a speedy riddance of all them that dwell in the land."

Zechariah 14:1-4 "Behold, the **day of the LORD** cometh, and thy spoil shall be divided in the midst of thee. [2]For I will gather all nations against Jerusalem to battle; and the city shall be taken, and the houses rifled, and the women ravished; and half of the city shall go forth into captivity, and the residue of the people shall not be cut off from the city. [3]Then shall the LORD go forth, and fight against those nations, as when he fought in the day of battle. [4]And his feet shall stand in that day upon the mount of Olives..." (obviously at the end of the week in fulfillment of Acts 1:11).

Malachi 4:5-6 "Behold, I will send you Elijah the prophet before the coming of the great and dreadful **day of the LORD**: [6]And he shall turn the heart of the fathers to the children, and the heart of the children to their fathers, lest I come and smite the earth with a curse."

Acts 2:19-21 "And I will show wonders in heaven above, and signs in the earth beneath; blood, and fire, and vapour of smoke: [20]The sun shall be turned into darkness, and the moon into blood, before that great and notable **day of the Lord** come: [21]And it shall come to pass, that whosoever shall call on the name of the Lord shall be saved" (note: v.20 speaks of the same cosmic events described in Matt. 24:28; Rev. 6:12-17; and Joel 3:12-15).

I Corinthians 5:1-5 "It is reported commonly that there is fornication among you, and such fornication as is not so much as named among the Gentiles, that one should have his father's wife. ²And ye are puffed up, and have not rather mourned, that he that hath done this deed might be taken away from among you. ³For I verily, as absent in body, but present in spirit, have judged already, as though I were present, concerning him that hath so done this deed, ⁴In the name of our Lord Jesus Christ, when ye are gathered together, and my spirit, with the power of our Lord Jesus Christ, ⁵To deliver such an one unto Satan for the destruction of the flesh, that the spirit may be saved in the **day of the Lord** Jesus."

II Corinthians 1:13-14 "For we write none other things unto you, than what ye read or acknowledge; and I trust ye shall acknowledge even to the end; ¹⁴As also ye have acknowledged us in part, that we are your rejoicing, even as ye also are ours in the **day of the Lord** Jesus."

I Thessalonians 5:1-4 "But of the times and the seasons, brethren, (of the resurrection and gathering of the saints) ye have no need that I write unto you. ²For yourselves know perfectly that the **day of the Lord** so cometh as a thief in the night. ³For when they shall say, Peace and safety; then sudden destruction cometh upon them, as travail upon a woman with child; and they shall not escape. ⁴But ye, brethren, are not in darkness, that that day should overtake you as a thief."

II Peter 3:10 "But the **day of the Lord** will come as a thief in the night; in the which the heavens shall pass away with a great noise, and the elements shall melt with fervent heat, the earth also and the works that are therein shall be burned up."

16

After reading and contemplating these verses, it is most natural to arrive at the conclusion, that the *"day of the Lord"* is not a good time for anyone, <u>except</u> for those who have been cleansed by the blood of Christ. It is a day that has been set aside for the punishment of the heathens: a day of God's extreme wrath when He punishes the world for their evil, and what they have done to His chosen people and for dividing up their land that God gave them. According to the scriptures presented, the day of the Lord, has the following characteristics or events:

- It is a time for the heathen
- It is a day of God's wrath and vengeance
- It is the time to *"punish the world for their evil"*
- *"the heavens shall be rolled together as a scroll"*
- It is His *"recompense for the controversy of Zion"*
- It is a *"day of darkness and gloominess...a day of clouds and thick darkness"*
- No one can stand or fight against *"that day"*
- Cosmic events will <u>precede</u> *"that day"*
- *"The whole land will be devoured by the fire of His jealousy"*
- Elijah will be sent to unite Israel <u>before</u> that day
- It will come *"suddenly"* and as a *"thief in the night"* (like the days of the Noahic flood)
- It is connected with the parousia of Christ (because of the cosmic events in Matt. 24:29)
- It's a day when the elements shall melt with the fervent heat with God's extreme wrath

There are also several other <u>direct</u> references to that day in the New Testament. They are:

<u>II Peter 3:12</u> "Looking for and hasting unto the coming (parousia) of the **day of God** wherein the heavens being on fire shall be dissolved, and the elements shall melt with fervent heat?"

<u>Philippians 1:6</u> "Being confident of this very thing, that he which hath begun a good work in you will perform it until the **day of Jesus Christ**..."

<u>Philippians 1:10</u> "That ye may approve things that are excellent; that ye may be sincere and without offence till the **day of Christ**..."

<u>II Thessalonians 2:2</u> "Now we beseech you, brethren, by the coming (parousia) of our Lord Jesus Christ, and by our gathering together unto Him, that ye be not soon shaken in mind, or be troubled, neither by spirit, nor by word, nor by letter as from us, as that the **day of Christ** is at hand."

<u>Revelation 6:16-17</u> "...And said to the mountains and rocks, fall on us, and hide us from the face of Him that sitteth on the throne, and from the wrath of the Lamb. [17]For **the great day of His wrath** is come: and who shall be able to stand?"

We see also a common and direct connection between the day of the Lord, His parousia, and the <u>cosmic events</u> that Jesus, John, Joel, and Isaiah wrote about. Let's look at those passages and compare their language (see also charts 10-14):

- Jesus, when discussing the subject of His parousia, said, *"Immediately <u>after</u> the tribulation of those days, shall* *the sun be darkened, and the moon shall not give her light, and the stars shall fall from heaven, and the powers of the heavens shall be shaken...and they shall see the Son of man coming in the clouds of heaven with power and great glory"* (Matt. 24:29-30 – compare the cosmic actions with the verbiage of: Isa. 13:10; Joel 2:10-11, 31, 3:15; Acts: 2:20; II Peter 3:9-10).

- John saw in his vision of the seals, *"And I beheld when he had opened the <u>sixth seal</u> and, lo, there was a great earthquake; and the sun became black as sackcloth of hair, and the moon became as blood; and the stars of heaven fell unto the earth, even as a fig tree casteth her untimely figs, when she is shaken of a mighty wind. And the heaven departed as a scroll when it is rolled together; and every mountain and island were moved out of their places"* (Rev. 6:12-14).

- Joel, a prophet, stated, *"The sun shall be turned into darkness, and the moon into blood, <u>before</u> the great and the terrible <u>day of the Lord</u> come...Put ye in the sickle, for the harvest is ripe: come, get ye down; for the press is full, the vats overflow; for their wickedness is great. Multitudes, multitudes in the valley of decision: for the <u>day of the Lord</u> is near in the valley of decision. The sun and the moon shall be darkened, and the stars shall withdraw their shining. The Lord also shall roar out of Zion, and utter His voice from Jerusalem; and the heavens and the earth shall shake..."* (Joel 2:31; 3:13-15).

- And then Isaiah speaks of that same event, *"Behold, the <u>day of the Lord</u> cometh...for the stars of heaven and the constellations thereof shall not give their light: the sun shall be darkened in his going forth, and the moon shall* *not cause her light to shine. And I will punish the world for their iniquity; and I will cause the arrogancy of the proud to cease..."* (Isa. 12:9a, 10-11).

- The entire 24th chapter of Isaiah speaks about the <u>day of the Lord's</u> judgment, and because of its intensity, I feel compelled to quote at least part of it, **"...for the windows from on high are open and the foundations of the earth do shake. The earth is utterly broken down, the earth is clean dissolved, the earth is moved exceedingly. The earth shall reel to and fro like a drunkard, and shall be removed like a cottage; and the transgression thereof shall be heavy upon it; and it shall fall, and not rise again. And it shall come to pass in that day that the Lord shall punish the host of the high ones that are on high** (angels)**, and the kings of the earth upon the earth...the moon shall be confounded and the sun ashamed..."** (Isa. 24:18b, 19-21. 23a).

Hal Lindsey, a pre-trib adherent and writer of prophecy books, believes the *"day of the Lord"* will begin <u>prior</u> to the start of the week. He states, *"The great falling away or apostasy of the professing Christian Church also takes place <u>before</u> the beginning of the tribulation which is sometimes called the <u>day of the Lord</u>"* *("The Rapture," 1983, Bantam Books, p.7)*. The *"day of the Lord"* is most definitely not interchangeable with the tribulation period, but is interchangeable with the wrath of God. Lindsey has placed many events to occur several literal weeks before the 70th week has even started (see chart #7). He removes the Holy Spirit, reveals Antichrist, has the 144,000 Jews witnessing, and starts the *"day of the Lord"* all before the 70th week even has even begun. In my opinion, to hold to such a position, you have to ignore many clear passages in the Word of God to come to such a conclusion. And, if the terrible wrath of God is meted out at the start of the week, then the results of His anger would certainly override all actions of Antichrist when he takes control and invades Jerusalem with his armies in the middle of the week (Lk. 21:20-22).

It should be reasonably evident that the start of the *"day of the Lord,"* the cosmic events, and the post-trib parousia of Matthew 24 all occur together or around the same time frame. Placing the *"day of the Lord"* in the beginning of the week, would seem to be a real stretch in light of the evidence. Whether or not the Day of the Lord is 24 hours, or one of an extended period of time, would have no bearing on when it starts. The first portion of the 70th week is a deceptive time of pseudo peace for Israel. The peace accord that is made between Israel and *"the many"* (Arab nations) and then *"confirmed"* (acknowledged and agreed to) by Antichrist, and is for 7 years (Dan. 9:27). Antichrist will break that accord in the middle, and wreak havoc from that time on until he is destroyed by the parousia of Christ (II Thess. 2:8). Wouldn't it seem logical, that if Antichrist breaks the treaty in the middle of the week by invading Jerusalem with his armies, that the time prior to that must have been reasonably peaceful, or at least that Israel had a perception of peace?

Daniel said, regarding the *"king of fierce countenance"* (Antichrist), *"24And his power shall be mighty, but not by his own power: and he shall destroy wonderfully* (by surprise, or suddenly), *and shall prosper, and practice, and shall destroy the mighty and the holy people. 25And through his policy also he shall Cause craft* (deceptive practices) *to prosper in his hand; and he shall magnify himself in his heart, and by peace shall destroy many: he shall also stand up against the Prince of princes* (Jesus Christ), *but he shall be broken without hand"* (not by natural causes or by man – Daniel 8:24-25). Antichrist comes to Israel with a betraying peace, but then in the middle of the 70th week when Satan empowers him, he will show his true colors and destructive power against the Jews and Christians, until the King of Kings comes from Heaven to destroy him and his powerful worldwide armies.

In light of the previous scriptures, we have directly connected the parousia (coming), the cosmic events, and the day of the Lord together. So, it would seem pre-mature and anti-climatic for God to judge the world, and cause all of these catastrophic events to be initiated at the beginning of the week. At that time, Antichrist hasn't even broken the peace accord, nor occupied the temple, nor has anyone received his name, mark, or number. The construction of the 3rd temple, and the revealing of Antichrist sitting in the temple as God, would have to be a sign prior to the coming of Christ; it would be difficult to abominate the temple if there was none. Paul clearly taught that the man of sin would be exposed <u>before</u> the gathering (rapture) of the believers (II Thess. 2:1-4). The Jews had to experience a re-gathering as a people and obtain a nation of their own, as well as have Jerusalem as their capital city. These things were prophesized in the Old Testament and would be signs to the Jews, because that is what they required. Remember, all prophecy is Jewish, but the Church has the benefit of watching their prophetic signs being fulfilled, much like the Church witnessed the prophetic destruction of Jerusalem in 70 A.D. in fulfillment of Daniel 9:26.

In charts #10-13, there are four sequences that are used to construct a case for a <u>scriptural</u> relationship between the <u>day of the Lord,</u> the <u>cosmic events</u>, the coming of <u>Elijah</u>, and the <u>great</u>

tribulation --- these relationships rest on solid ground. The time line has no reference to the 70th week in these charts, but show the relationship to one another. It is much easier to establish when these events transpire, than to debate, with much aggravation, the rapture location. But once these events are thought through, they paint a pretty good picture of where the rapture can't be. Sometimes it is easier to construct portions of a model by eliminating where an event can't be, rather then attempting to place them it in an ambiguous location. After studying these charts, it will be easier to establish the position of the rapture and to show why it must be placed between the 6th and 7th seal. This thought is more in agreement with the single parousia which Jesus and His Apostles taught, as opposed to developing a model with two comings. Paul stated, concerning our resurrection and the timing of it, *"23But every man in his own order: Christ the first fruits; afterward they that are Christ's at His coming, 24a then cometh the end, when he shall have delivered up the kingdom to God..."* (I Cor. 15:23, 24a). Once more, the reference to *"His coming,"* implies a single coming, not two.

Again, the main focus on charts (#10-13), is the relationship of the events to one another, and not where they occur in the week. Both the pre-wrath and the author's post-trib model, agree in this relationship, but see a difference as to where the 6th seal ends (see charts 6, 8). It would be difficult to defend the idea, that the cosmic events described by Peter, John, Paul, Isaiah, and Jesus are unrelated and occur at different times. Think about it, how many times can the stars fall to the earth? --- this is the beginning of God's extreme wrath! If John said the cosmic events happen at the sixth seal (Rev. 6:12-17), and Jesus said these same cosmic events happen immediately after the great tribulation (Mt. 24:29), then how can the rapture occur in the beginning of the week, unless the 6th seal is placed there also? And if the 6th seal did transpire at the beginning, then the other 5 seals would be outside of the week, and the great tribulation would be also. None of that would make sense! I have never had any serious resistance to the thought that these cosmic events are the same, occurring only once. They are not 4 different cosmic events.

The main purpose of the day of the Lord is to punish the wicked who have rejected and blasphemed Christ. We know that even in the days of the tribulation, there are people who curse God and shake their fist at Him. After God's various plagues, the nations were angry with God because of the pain that the two witnesses caused and the plagues that He delivered upon them (Rev. 9:20; 11:17; 16:8-11). Isaiah said it well, *"Let favor be shown to the wicked, yet he will not learn righteousness: in the land of uprightness will he deal unjustly, and will not behold the majesty of the Lord"* (Isa. 26:10).

The next chart, #14, says the same thing as charts #10-13, but arranged slightly different. Once more, we can plainly see the same cosmic events occur:

1. before the day of the Lord,
2. at the opening of the 6th seal
3. immediately after the great tribulation.

We see that Malachi, Isaiah, Joel, Zechariah, John, and Jesus are all describing the exact same thing, which fits together perfectly, revealing to us exactly where the gathering of the "elect" is (Mt. 24:29). The Day of the Lord cannot possibly transpire at the beginning of the week.

One further comment on the *"day of the Lord."* Elijah is

forecasted to come <u>before</u> that day. Malachi said, *"⁵Behold, I will send you Elijah the prophet <u>before</u> the coming of the great and terrible day of the Lord: ⁶and he shall turn the heart of the fathers to children, and the heart of the children to the fathers, lest I come and smite the earth with a curse"* (Mal. 3:5-6). That certainly would be a "sign" if you place the day of the Lord at the beginning, thereby casting more suspicion on imminency. Lindsey probably viewed that as a problem, and placed the rapture and other events several weeks prior to the start of the week to avoid the dilemma.

(2) End of the Age and the Time of Harvest

Jesus has said to His Church, *"...and lo I am with you always, even unto the <u>end of the world</u>"* (age - Mt. 28:20). If you believe Christ comes at the beginning of the week, then the end of the age and the time of the final harvest must be placed there; this would appear to be illogical. The process of severing the wicked from the just is the final separation (harvest) of the living saints from the unsaved heathen that are alive in that day. This event appears to be occurring at the beginning of the kingdom, not at the beginning of the week – you plant in the spring and harvest in the fall! But perhaps you may be thinking, *"Jesus was referring to the end of the Church age, and that ends at the beginning of the week."* We must remember that the "tares" (wicked) are gathered "<u>first</u>" and then the wheat (believers) is gathered into the barn; but how could this be so, if the wheat was gathered first at the beginning of the week? (Matthew 13:30, 39-41).

The "<u>end of the age</u>" and the "<u>end of the "Church age</u>" are one and the same. I am a dispensationalist to an extent, and do believe that the treatment of Israel and the Church are somewhat different; but when it is held that the Church cannot be present in the 70th week, that presents a problem. When Jesus said, *"Lo, I will be with you always even unto the end of the world"* (Mt. 28:20), He meant exactly that --- at the end of the history of man. It would seem natural to include the last 7 years of mans control, and the binding of Satan, which is just before Christ takes the reigns and rules with a rod of iron. The *"end of the world"* does not happen at the <u>beginning</u> of the week; there is no biblical support for such a thought. The *"fullness of the Gentiles"* marks the end of the age, a period of time of mans rule (Ro. 11:25). You might say that it parallels the *"last days,"* where Peter was talking, in context, about the parousia of Christ (II Pet. 3.3). The real question here is, can the Church, biblically, be in the 70th week at the same time as Israel. Pre-tribbers will say that the Church wasn't present during Daniel's prophecy because the prophecy was Jewish in nature; therefore the Church cannot be there. That sounds reasonable, and the premise might be correct, but the conclusion is flawed and not supported by scripture. First of all, the "Church," as we use the term today, did not come into existence until Pentecost, and therefore couldn't be in the Old Testament; but now, the Church does exist and can be in the 70th week. Daniel prophesied of 70 weeks of years, or 490 years, (Dan. 9:24) before Israel would enter the physical kingdom. Futurists believe that 69 of those weeks of years have already been fulfilled, with a pause between the 69th week and the 70th. Two main prophesied events have occurred <u>after</u> the 69 weeks: (1) Jesus was cut off (crucified), and (2) Jerusalem was destroyed in 70 AD. by the Roman army under General Titus (Dan. 9:26). While that particular Jewish prophecy was being fulfilled (e.g. - Dan. 9:26), the Church had already been in existence for almost <u>40 years</u>, and co-existing with Israel. The truth is, that Jewish prophecy was predicted in Daniel's day, but fulfilled in the Church age. So, when the 70th week of Jewish prophecy is being fulfilled, once again the Church will be co-existing with Israel; there is no scriptural support or reason to exclude the Church from it. The 70th week is a transitional time for the Jews and they will remain in the Church age until their Messiah comes. No scripture ends the Church age prior to the harvest when the wicked are separated from the just. The Christians will be cleansed and made ready for reigning over the unsaved world (there will be lots of unsaved people entering into the millennial kingdom, and Jesus will be ruling with a <u>rod of iron</u> during that time and we will be co-reigning with Him – Rev. 2:27; 12:5; 19:15; Ps. 2:9; Zec. 14:16, etc.).

Paul made a statement while speaking to the saints, saying, *"<u>If we suffer</u>, we shall reign with Him: if we deny Him, He will also deny us"* (II Tim 2:12). And then immediately after they had stoned Paul and left him for dead, he got up and went back into the city and our text says, *"Confirming the souls of the disciples, and exhorting them to continue in the faith, and that we must, through <u>much tribulation</u>, enter into the kingdom of God."* (Acts 14:22). That tribulation is confirmed by John while writing about the saints at the end of the tribulation period, saying, *"These are they which came out of <u>great tribulation</u>, and have washed their robes, and made them white in the blood of the Lamb"* (Rev. 7:14). These Christians may have had "dirty" robes like many of us do today, meaning that we are sometimes involved in worldly things and shouldn't be. We generally live like feeble, weak kneed Christians and a good dose of tribulation would surely clean up our dirty white robes. When it comes to Christians having great tribulation in their lives, there is no shortage of examples in scripture and in real life today around the world, particularly in the Islamic countries. Can the great tribulation be any worse for the saints than the horrors and tortures of the reformation period? – or the despicable acts of torture under the Roman emperors, Hitler and others of their kind. Paul said, *"¹⁸For I reckon that the <u>sufferings</u> of this present time are not worthy to be compared with the glory which shall be revealed in us... ²⁵Thrice was I beaten with rods, once was I stoned, thrice I suffered shipwreck, a night and a day I have been in the deep...* (Ro. 8:18, II Cor. 11:25). What promise is there anywhere in the Bible that tells us that we will escape trials, testings, and the tribulation? Unfortunately, these are what make us strong, and gives God the glory that is rightfully His. It was Christ who suffered and died for us, so why do we think that God will not allow us to experience persecution like all of the rest of the saints in history? Are we that righteous? – I don't think so!

In Matthew, chapter 13, the wheat and tares parable, Jesus spoke to the Jewish multitude and afterwards gave a private interpretation of the parable to His Apostles. The interpretation was a picture of the judgment of the wicked (Satan's children) and a separation of the righteous (the wheat). The separating will be done at the end of the world (age). The exact words of Christ are, *"⁴⁹So shall it be at the <u>end of the world</u>: the <u>angels</u> shall come forth, and sever the wicked from the just, ⁵⁰and shall cast them into the furnace of fire: there shall be weeping and gnashing of teeth"* (Matt. 13:49-50). The tares (heathen) are gathered <u>first,</u> and then the wheat (God's people) are gathered. *"...Let them both grow together until the harvest; and in the time of the harvest I will say to the reapers, gather ye together <u>first the tares</u>, and bind them in bundles to burn them; but gather the <u>wheat</u> into My barn"* (Mt. 13:30). If you place

28

the rapture at the beginning of the week, then the angels must come at that time in secret, because that's what the pre-tribbers believe, that is, the rapture is silent, secret, and without signs. In reason, however, it would seem more likely, that the wicked will be removed by God's judgment via the final vials (bowls) and the battle of Armageddon at the time of harvest (Joel 3:9-17). Then the children of the kingdom (Abraham's seed of the promise) will go into their permanent kingdom forever (Joel 3:20). We must remember all prophecy is related to the Jews in the Old Testament. When the wicked are destroyed, then the Jews, the apple of God's eye (Zech. 2:8), will live in peace and safety fulfilling the prophecy of the wheat and the tares. They will reproduce, plant vineyards, build houses, etc. (Ezek. 28:26, Isa. 65: 20-21). They will not have glorified bodies like we will, but will live forever because of their partaking of the *"trees of life"* which will be on the both sides of the river flowing from the temple to the Dead Sea (which will be healed and have great numbers of fish – Ezek. 47:7-12). At the start of the millennium, when Jesus is sitting on His throne in Israel, the 12 Apostles will be given the position as leaders and judges over the 12 tribes of Israel (Mt. 19:28; Lk. 22:30). The Church will be ruling and reigning with Christ, in glorified bodies, over the leftover surviving Gentiles (Rev. 3:21, 12:5, 19:15, 20:4). This then, is truly a dispensational setting in a setting of Jewish prophecy. We must remember that when Jesus came, He came as a prophet, a priest, and King, but they wouldn't let Him be their king – so that's the purpose of the kingdom, to fulfill Jewish prophecy with Jesus Christ as their King. God's chosen ones will one day be without persecution from any nation or people, while the wicked will be their servants for a thousand years before they are brought to eternal justice (Zeph. 3:13-15; Isa. 14:2; 49:22-23; 54:3; 60:14; Jer. 12-17).

It is interesting to note, that in the same parable of the wheat and tares, the <u>angels</u> are doing the harvesting and separating. We read of a harmonizing description of the same harvest by John in Revelation, *"¹⁵And another <u>angel</u> came out of the temple, crying with a loud voice to Him that sat on the cloud, thrust in thy sickle, and reap: for <u>the time is come for thee to reap</u>; for the <u>harvest</u> of the earth is ripe. ¹⁶ And he that sat on the cloud thrust in his sickle on the earth; and <u>the earth was reaped</u> ...¹⁹and the <u>angel</u> thrust in his sickle into the earth, and gathered the vine of the earth, and cast it into the great winepress of the wrath of God"* (Rev. 14:15-16, 19). This angel followed another angel who warned the inhabitants of the earth not to take the mark, his name, or worship the image of the beast (Antichrist), therefore we know that the harvest cannot be in the beginning of the week because the angel is warning inhabitants of the earth not to take the mark or worship Antichrist's image which is sometime after the middle of the week. The harvest is <u>after</u> the great tribulation. And again, Paul writes about the reaping, *"...⁷The Lord Jesus shall be revealed from heaven <u>with His mighty angels</u>, ⁸in flaming fire taking vengeance on them that know not God, and that obey not the gospel of our Lord Jesus Christ: ⁹who shall be punished with everlasting destruction from the presence of the Lord and from the glory of His power..."* (I Thess. 1:7-9). And we have Joel, in chapter 3, relating the same harvest, he says, *"¹³Put ye in the sickle, for the harvest is ripe: come, get you down; for the press is full, the vats overflow; for their wickedness is great. ¹⁴Multitudes, multitudes in the valley of decision: for the <u>day of the LORD</u> is near in the valley of decision. ¹⁵The sun and the moon* *shall be darkened, and the stars shall withdraw their shining"* (vs. 13-15 – notice where the day of the Lord is; this is more proof that the end-time harvest cannot be at the beginning of the week).

A question that should arise for pre-tribulationists is how many times does Jesus come with His angels in great power and glory? At the post-trib parousia Jesus comes with His angels (Mt. 24:29). Does it not seem plausible that the harvest would take place at the end of the week where the wicked are gathered and destroyed first and then the righteous shine forth (Mt. 13:41). It has been suggested that since the angels are not present in the "rapture" text of I Thess. 4, that there must be two different phases of His coming. But that argument is weak because the angels are not present when Paul talks about "... *our gathering together unto Him"* (rapture) in II Thess. 2:1. So, every time his "coming" is mentioned in scripture, the context doesn't necessarily demand that angels be present, and in many parousia texts, angels are not mentioned. We have just shown that the angels (reapers) are present at the end of the age, and that is when Jesus said He will be with us, but pre-trib adherents must place the end of the world (age) at the beginning of the week which again, has the righteous gathered first, and then the wicked, just the opposite of what Jesus said in Matthew 13.

I think, that after serious consideration, it could be agreed upon that the time of the final harvest, and the end of the age belong at the end of the week or just before the kingdom setup; and to suggest that the "Church age" ends at the beginning of the week, in light of the revealed scripture, would be a difficult notion to accept; especially since there will be millions of Christians present during the tribulation who won't take the mark, name, or the number of the Antichrist. John reveals, *"Here is the patience of the <u>saints</u>; here are they that keep the commandments of God, and the faith of Jesus"* (Rev. 14:12). *"and I saw the souls of them that were beheaded for <u>the witness of Jesus</u> and for the word of God, and had not worshipped the beast, neither his image, neither had received his mark upon their foreheads, or in their hands; and they lived and reigned with Christ a thousand years"* (Rev. 20:4b). That description was one of the *"First resurrection."* It would seem to me, that if there was some other time of the *"first resurrection,"* besides the one at the end of the great tribulation, then we should read about it somewhere. To conclude that the Christians who go through the tribulation, and that these first resurrection martyrs are not a part of the Church, would be a contradiction of the facts presented. *"For where two or three are gathered together in My name, there am I in the midst of them"* (Mt. 18:20). It certainly appears that the Church is present in the 70th week, right up to the very end when the parousia of Christ occurs.

The Rapture of the Church
(secret, silent and without signs)

> *"[16]For this we say unto you by the word of the Lord, that we which are alive and remain unto the coming (Grk. – parousia) of the Lord shall not prevent (go before) them which are asleep. [16]For the Lord Himself shall descend from heaven <u>with a shout</u>, with <u>the voice of the archangel,</u> and with <u>the trump of God</u>: and the dead in Christ shall rise first: [17]then we which are alive and remain shall be caught up (raptured) together with them in the clouds, to meet the Lord in the air: and so shall we ever be with the Lord. [18]Wherefore comfort one another with these words. [1]But of the times and the sea-*

sons brethren, ye have no need that I write unto you. ²For yourselves know perfectly that the <u>day of the Lord</u> so cometh as a thief in the night. ³For when they shall say, Peace and safety; then sudden destruction cometh upon them, as travail upon a woman with child; and they shall not escape. ⁴But ye brethren <u>are not</u> in darkness, that that day should overtake you as a thief" (I Thess. 4:16-18; 5:1-4).

"¹Now we beseech you, brethren, by the <u>coming</u> (parousia) of the Lord Jesus Christ, and by our <u>gathering together</u> (rapturing) unto Him, ²that ye be not soon shaken in mind, or be troubled, neither by spirit, nor by word, nor by letter as from us, as that the day of Christ is at hand. ³Let no man deceive you by any means: for <u>that day</u> (day of the Lord) shall not come, except there come a falling away first, and that man of sin be revealed, the son of perdition (Antichrist); ⁴who opposeth and exalteth himself above all that is called God, or that is worshipped; so that he as God sitteth in the temple of God shewing himself that he is God" (II Thess. 2:1-4).

The above two texts are the only clear "rapture" passages in the Word of God referring directly to the "<u>catching up</u>" or the "<u>gathering together of the saints.</u>" Both texts deal with Christ's parousia and the timing of the event in relation to the day of the Lord. Some would argue that John 14:1-3, is a rapture text also that deals in the timing, and it certainly is a passage on the coming of Christ but does not relate in any way to the timing of the rapture, stating only that we will be with Christ wherever He is. If you do consider this passage to be a rapture text, there is no stated relationship to the timing of it, in reference to the week or the day of the Lord.

The doctrine of a "secret, silent, coming" of Christ for His Church, is a major departure from the written records and testimonies of the early Church, and Church witnesses down through centuries. We should view the "rapture" as part of the "coming" (parousia) of Christ. In other words, at the *"coming,"* of Christ, we will be raptured or resurrected, and it only happens once. There is no other coming! (scripture clearly states that Jesus comes after the great tribulation). Jesus came once to make atonement for our sins, and then He will come again a second time to complete our glorification by making us to be without sin.

If there was a difference between the post-tribulation coming (parousia) that Christ taught, and some other earlier one, it would have been in these two rapture texts; otherwise the disciples would have been confused by what Paul was now teaching. Here Paul is clearly teaching that the *"gathering together"* (rapture) couldn't happen until the man of sin was revealed sitting in the temple as God. So, let's examine in a few words this "secret silent rapture" theory, and see how it became a different event than the post-trib "parousia" that Jesus talked about (Matt. 24:28).

First, I wish to note several facts regarding the above two rapture texts:

- It is the coming of Christ (Grk.-parousia)
- Christ descends from heaven with a shout (not silent or secret)
- There is the voice of the archangel (not silent or secret)
- The trumpet of God sounds (not silent or secret)
- Christians will not be in the dark when the day of the Lord is about to materialize

- A falling away from the faith occurs <u>prior</u> to the day of the Lord

- The Antichrist is manifested, sitting in the temple as God, <u>before</u> the day of the Lord

- Christ's parousia has a direct connection with the day of the Lord (not silent or secret)

Viewing chart #2, we see the various "<u>rapture</u>" locations within the <u>pre-millennial</u> model. It should be noted that the pre-millennial view is a <u>Futurist</u> position (author), believing that most of the book of Revelation and some prophecy in Daniel is yet future, as opposed to Historicism, or Preterism (see glossary). <u>Preterists</u> view the *"last days"* as the last days of the Mosaic covenant and not the last day of God's dealing with man. They believe that Christ has already come and raised the dead with all prophecy fulfilled at or before the destruction of Jerusalem in 70 A.D.. They believe Paradise has been restored in Christ (spiritually speaking) and that all of His enemies have been conquered. We find that most Preterists are amillennialists or post-millennialists. <u>Historicists</u> on the other hand, view the book of Revelation as a past and present history of the Church from the time the N.T. was written, until the 2nd advent, yet future. To them, they see Antichrist as: the papacy, the "man of sin" in II Thessalonians, and the beast in Revelation 13.

In chart #2, there are located the various rapture locations in relation to the 70th week. One of those is the mid-trib position (I have never personally met a person that holds to that position). Probably the most well known adherent of this view would be Dr. Gleason Archer, professor of Old Testament at Trinity Evangelical Divinity School. He has co-authored a book, published by Zondervan, 1984, entitled, *"The Rapture Pre,-mid,- or*

Post Tribulational." The book holds a debate between the three positions with Dr. Paul Feinberg, a pre-trib believer (also from the same school), and Dr. Douglas Moo (same school) who is a post-trib believer. They give their views and responses with rebuttals after each has presented their views. Archer tries to blend in the two other positions and take advantage of the weaknesses in both positions. The mid-trib position was first introduced in about 1947.

The pre-wrath position (chart #6) is held by Marvin Rosenthal, executive director of Zion's Hope ministry in Orlando, Florida and editor of Zion's Fire (a Christian outreach to the Jewish people). He published a book in 1990, entitled, *"The Pre-wrath Rapture of the Church,"* a position, which in my opinion, is much closer to a post-trib scenario than any pre-trib or mid-trib model. If Mr. Rosenthal did not believe the trumpets followed the seals, rather than have them somewhat concurrent, his position would be, very close to the authors post-trib model (chart #8). I personally consider his position to be correct regarding the relationship between: the day of the Lord, the great tribulation, the cosmic events, and the resurrection (rapture). The difference is where you place the 7th trumpet and the 6th and 7th seals; and as an added plug for Mr. Rosenthal, I must quote his feelings on the rapture issue and the difficulty that he had in crossing over after being pre-trib for over 35 years. In his book,

"The Pre-wrath Rapture of the Church," he expresses his deep concern for his brethren by saying, *"...I was an uncompromising pre-tribulationist. But through many more months of conversation and biblical investigation, something began to happen. I can only describe it by saying that I believe the Spirit of God began to sow a seed of honest inquiry in my heart. Was it possible? Could it be?*

36

Notwithstanding my earnestness and sincerity, was I proclaiming a concept which the Bible did not substantiate? Was I prescribing a false hope? Could I be dispensing candy-coated pills that tasted good but did no good? And in the doing, was I keeping from God's children a medicine that would truly help? Was I, however unintentionally, misinterpreting a considerable body of truth, truth that God intended to be a catalyst for holy living at all times and of paramount importance for the generation of believers that will, in fact, move into the seventieth week of the book of Daniel? The very thought troubled me. Of this I was certain: I could not be passive on this question. I would have to go back and reexamine the biblical basis for my pre-tribulation position and, while I was at it, the mid- and post-tribulation positions as well" (p.19). Knowing Mr. Rosenthal personally, and his high moral character, I can sympathize with those feelings. It took a lot of courage for a man in his position to make that change. As another note, relating to the high cost of switching positions, there was a very well known author who wrote a series of books and made a personal attack, in writing, upon Rosenthal in an attempt to belittle his new view. That was below the belt and uncalled for; any author who ridicules another brother and attacks his character personally should hold his head in shame. We may have our disagreements in the elements of eschatology, but our love for one another trumps all of the commandments, so let's exhibit that love and be respectful, not letting our tongue manifest unruly evil. James has said it well, *"⁵ Even so the tongue is a little member, and boasteth great things. Behold, how great a matter a little fire kindleth! And the tongue is a fire, a world of iniquity: so is the tongue among our members, that it defileth the whole body, and setteth on fire the course of nature; and it is set on fire of hell"* (James 3:5-6).

Concerning the birth of the "secret silent rapture" I will not go into the background or enter into the debate of <u>Margaret McDonald</u>, other than to say that she was a charismatic Scottish girl who had visions and trances at the age of 15. She was born about 1815, and reportedly one day had a vision of a distinction between the "caching up" of the saints and the second advent. Her story is several pages long so it will not be printed here. Suffice to say, she was influential in the beginnings of the dispensational theology and the "any moment" return of Christ. She had also shared her vision of her "secret, silent, resurrection" of the Church with <u>Edward Irving</u> (1792-1834 - a charismatic, tongues speaking, theologian from Scotland, who then proposed it as a <u>new</u> doctrine at a prophecy conference in Dublin, Ireland in 1830). It is not my intent to use this information to belittle the sources, but to give the facts as to the origination of the recent pre-tribulation theory. There is a fountain of documented information in the <u>public libraries</u> and on Wikipedia, to research Edward Irving's enormous influence on the "any moment" rapture theory, as well as Margaret McDonald's.

It was <u>John Nelson Darby</u> (1801-1882) who was credited as being the father of "dispensationalism" and how it is viewed today. The view of a "secret silent rapture" was later advanced by certain pre-millennialists at the Niagara Bible Conference (1878-1900) in New York. That conference popularized the pre-millennial doctrine in North America, and held a futurists perspective, but also had attendee's that were historicists. The rapture debate was an issue in the conference during the late 1880's. It was after the death of some of the founding men that the pre-tribulation position of an "any moment" rapture advanced. It should be noted that in the beginning of the conference, a "two stage" parousia was not held. Article 2 used the terms "glorious epiphany," "visible bodily return to this earth," and "this blessed hope," interchangeably as one and the same event. There was also great debate over the meaning of the word "imminent." The conference eventually died out in 1909, and shortly after that, Gaebelein and Cyrus Scofield started the Sea Cliff Bible Conference on Long Island, NY (my old stomping grounds) but the viewpoints held by the attendee's were entirely pre-tribulation. The funding for the startup of Sea Cliff came from some wealthy members of the Plymouth Brethren ("follow the money" – so, now we know!). This information was gleaned from Richard Reiter, co-author of *"The Rapture -Pre,-Mid,-or Post-Tribulational"* 1984, Zondervan, who did a fantastic job of documenting the advancement of the pre-millennial position in reference to the Niagara Bible Conference. A further detailed study on the development of the various pre-millennial positions, as written by Reiter, is highly recommended.

Cyrus Scofield (1841-1923) produced the Scofield Reference Bible, which was first published in 1909. It became the strongest influence in North America popularizing the highly dispensational "secret silent rapture" theory, via his internal notes. He also became the pastor of D. L. Moody's church and was in charge of Moody's Bible Training School further influencing the pre-trib theory. It was R.A. Torrey (1856-1928), who actually became the superintendent of that school in 1889 (later to become known as the Moody Bible Institute). Along with Scofield and Torrey, at the turn of the century era, were others like: Gaebelein, James Gray (also at the Moody Bible Institute), Dr. Harry Ironside, and L.S. Chafer, and others who were pre-trib in their conviction. And since then, the Church in America has be inundated with mostly fictional novels promoting the

39

theme of a secret silent rapture, and advancing the idea that those who missed the "first rapture flight," and were left behind at the first stage, could catch another flight at the second stage, so to speak. In other words, they would get a second chance, and if they did somehow become Christians, they would live in mortal bodies, with I Cor. 15:51-52 having no effect on them. In my thinking, nothing could be more devastating, then to mislead those whose soul is at risk of damnation by teaching them that they could have another chance. How many people today, might think, *"if this Bible stuff is really true, then I'll believe it later when I see the rapture thing."* Jesus has said, *"...Behold, now is the accepted time; behold, now is the day of salvation"* (II Cor. 6:2). One might ask what passage in scripture supports or alludes to a "second" chance for salvation after they have heard the Gospel and refused to believe? I find only scriptures of caution to the contrary, such as, *"[10]And with all deceivableness of unrighteousness in them that perish; because they received not the love of the truth, that they might be saved. [11]And for this cause God shall send them strong delusion, that they should believe a lie: [12]that they all might be damned who believed not the truth, but had pleasure in unrighteousness"* (II Thess. 2:10-12). Do those words of Paul sound like a "second chance" for those who heard the Gospel message and refused to believe? Can we find anyplace in scripture that teaches dogmatically, that any soul gets saved during the great tribulation? Did anyone get a 2nd chance in the flood? Did anyone get a 2nd chance in Sodom and Gomorrah? All I can find is the statement by John, *"[12]Here is the patience of the saints: here are they that keep the commandments of God, and the faith of Jesus. [13]And I heard a voice from heaven saying unto me, Write, Blessed are the dead which die in the Lord from henceforth: Yea, saith the*

Spirit, that they may rest from their labours; and their works do follow them" (Rev. 14:12-13). These are part of the saints who stand before the throne of God as recorded in Revelation 7:9.

It wasn't until about the late 1980's and early 1990's that the "secret silent rapture" pre-trib theory was seriously challenged, and is growing stronger even as I write this treatise. Most of the older seasoned pastors who went to seminaries were taught a two coming or "two phase" any moment secret silent rapture, and there was not much resistance from the young pastors, nor was there time to seriously <u>study</u> the many pertinent passages in the O.T. and N.T.. The secret silent rapture theory was preached and taught in the 50's and on through the 80's, and still is, but seemed to have lost a lot of its force lately. As a result of this re-examination, little serious preaching or Bible teaching on the subject has been done, and I don't mean the lone teaching of the pre-trib theory, but the other positions as well. There may be some very dear Christians who will never change their views because of the material that they have already published, or have preached (Jesus would have to speak to them personally). They feel they would be hurting their congregations if they revealed something else other than that which they have taught. But is that really what God would want? Isn't it better to be unassuming and simply say to them, that after re-examining scripture, the Holy Spirit has brought to light a clearer position regarding the timing of Christ's return? Is there not a responsibility to God's people as shepherd's of God's flock? The path to the truth must be held in high esteem. Solomon said, *"When pride cometh, then cometh shame: but with the lowly is wisdom"* (Proverbs 11:2). It certainly is not a shame to change ones mind on a subject that is very complex and engulfs a significant volume of scripture. When emerging from the reformation, look at all of the papal baggage the reformers carried with them: baby baptism, Christ present in the elements, baptism as a necessity for salvation, double predestination, etc.. Let us not also come out of the 21st century with our suitcases full of erroneous unsubstantiated "hand me downs" from the 21st century.

"Looking for that blessed hope, and the <u>glorious appearing</u> of the great God and our Saviour, Jesus Christ" (Titus 2:13 - as an interesting side note, the NASB, which follows the Catholic text, says that we are looking for the *"appearing of His glory,"* which is a clear reflection of Gnosticism and affecting the deity of Christ - one portrays Christ's physical return, and the other His spiritual return). It seems a shame that many Christians are not tremendously enthusiastic about an impending event that will rock the planet and change everything. We sing the songs that relate to that glorious moment when we shall all be changed from mortal to immortal. This subject should not be abandoned, but rather studied all the more as we see the day of His coming approaching. In today's environment many Christians are discouraged, having seen the morals and values plummet in America. And sometimes it seems hopeless to stem the tide of materialism with the cornucopia of goods that are flashed before our eyes. The passionate message of Calvary, and the return of Christ, in America, is competing with the internet, the MP-3's, I-pods, cell phones, DVD's, movies, Plasma TV's, new automobiles, boats, campers and all of the latest technological junk that launches us into a stupor, and hinders the Gospel from being received by people who need it the most. So let us not cast off or discard the study of the *"... the things which shall be hereafter"* (Rev. 1:19); if we do, the magnificent

picture that has been so clearly portrayed and impressed upon the mind of John, and the things that Jesus has promised the believer, will fade – and that would be so sad. We need to get back to the basics with individual discipleship by focusing on the cross, the resurrection, and the return of Christ, thus producing a generation of believers living holy lives. You cannot teach the broad subject of eschatology (another scholars fancy word for future things to come), without teaching the death, burial, and resurrection of Christ.

It was John that quoted the words of Jesus, *"Blessed is he that <u>readeth</u>, and they that <u>hear</u> the words of this prophecy, and keep those things which are written therein: for the time is at hand"* (Rev. 1:3) A few verses later John declared, *"Behold, He cometh* (parousia) *with clouds; and every eye shall see Him, and they also which pierced Him: and all kindreds of the earth shall wail because of Him..."* (v.7). We need to visualize in our minds His appearing with the angels and the souls of the saints that Jesus will bring with Him to reunite with their decayed bodies. Have you ever mentally pictured the coming of Christ with His angels and the saints? How brilliant the sky will be, and what a breathtaking experience that will be! The songwriter, James Black, wrote of that day in an old familiar tune, *"<u>When the Roll is Called up Yonder:</u>"*

"When the trumpet of the Lord shall sound and time shall be no more
And the morning breaks eternal, bright and fair;
When the saved on earth shall gather over on the other shore,
And the roll is called up yonder, I'll be there.

On that bright and cloudless morning when
    the dead in Christ will rise,
And the morning of His resurrection share;

When His chosen ones shall gather to their home beyond the skies,
And the roll is called up yonder, I'll be there.

Let us labor for the Master from the dawn till setting sun;
Let us talk of all His wondrous love and care;
Then when all of life is over and our work on earth is done,
And the roll is called up yonder, I'll be there."

Another song that reminds of us of the parousia of Christ was written by Carl Blackmore, entitled, "*Some Golden Daybreak.*"

"Some glorious morning, sorrow will cease,
Some glorious morning all will be peace;
Heartaches all ended, labor all done,
Heaven will open and Jesus will come.

Sad hearts will gladden, all shall be bright,
Good-bye for ever to earth's dark night;
Changed in a moment, like Him to be,
Oh, glorious day-break, Jesus I'll see.

Oh, what a meeting, there in the skies,
No tears nor crying shall dim our eyes;
Loved ones united eternally,
Oh, what a day-break that morning will be.

Some golden day-break Jesus will come;
Some golden day-break, battles all won,
He'll shout the victory, break through the blue,
Some golden day-break for me, for you."

Another song that touched the heart of very dear friend of mine, shortly after he was led to Christ, was written by Eugene Barnett in 1939. It tells the Gospel story from the beginning to the end, entitled, "*Victory in Jesus*"

"I heard an old, old story, how a Saviour came from glory,
How He gave His life on Calvary to save a wretch like me;
I heard about His groaning, of His precious blood's atoning,
Then I repented of my sins and won the victory.

I heard about His healing, of His cleansing power revealing,
How He made the lame to walk again and caused the blind to see;
Then I cried, Dear Jesus, come and heal my broken spirit,
And somehow Jesus came and brought to me the victory.

I heard about a mansion He has built for me in glory,
And I heard about the streets of gold beyond the crystal sea;
About the angels singing, and the old redemption story,
And some sweet day I'll sing up there, the song of victory."

I miss the songs of old! I love the words, the messages, and the stories behind those old hymns, the ones that testified of Calvary, the blood, their labors, and of the coming of our Saviour. Many of these songwriters were penning their songs while under torture or duress, or just plain old discouragement, yet others wrote while on a spiritual high. It is a sad thing that modern day "worship" songs have taken the place of some of these old flagships. Not that the new overheads are "bad," or are deficient in their message, but rather that many congregations have discarded the old for the new to satisfy the "new breed" of worshippers today, many of who just want to "feel good." These new praise and worship songs also relieve us from the old "bloody" hymns that are so offensive. Many of those new tunes are not easy to learn and sing as a congregation, and many times they are sung with very loud volume with drums and electronic amplification making it not very pleasant to the ears and difficult to concentrate on the words of the song. If you took away the overheads, there would be very little movement on the lips of the people in the congregation. And of course, let us not forget the $millions$ that are collected from the copyrighted material, CD's, downloads, etc.. There's not much profit in the old "public domain" hymns. The same goes for all of the "new and improved" Bibles—copyrighted Bibles mean $$$.

During Christmas of 2006, my wife and I had a Christian family from England come and visit us; they had miniscule teaching about any of the details surrounding the return of Christ – I was appalled! They have been saved and serving for years. What has happened to the pastors who are supposed to preach the "whole Word?" In my opinion many good pastors and Bible teachers may be having a confidence crisis regarding their views in eschatology, and that they are not as well versed on the subject as they would like to be. As a result, the Church suffers, and is anemic regarding the parousia of Christ, and so many other exciting details about our future and that of Israel, the apple of His eye.

As I look back, and having sat in many Bible believing churches over the last 50 years, I can't ever recall hearing a sermon on the *"day of the Lord;"* not even one! Why is that? Nor have I heard about the numerous specific blessings that Israel will receive during the kingdom period. And when the book of Revelation is preached, it is often taught that the seven churches are different periods of Church history and accompanying dates are given for each period. This teaching, by its very essence, presents difficulty for a pre-tribulation parousia; how could Christ have come back in an earlier time period, if all of the 7 Church periods hadn't come to pass yet? And besides, even if they were church periods, who determines when they start and when they end? And of course, if Israel wasn't a nation until 1948, and Jerusalem, which was re-captured in 1967, wasn't their capital city, then Christ couldn't have come back any time prior to that date without having a sign that indicated that we were close to the end of the age.

For almost 1800 years, the general Christian Church teaching and written historical records have held that the Church would go through a time of tribulation before the parousia of Christ, and that they would see the *"man of sin"* (Antichrist) arriving on the scene. The Church never saw two future comings of Christ, and to suggest that it was a common teaching of the past, would be untruthful. Even if you found a person or two who vaguely mentioned two future comings, it certainly was not the general belief of the historical Church. The question is, what does the scripture teach and what do the majority of Church records reveal of past history regarding a two stage parousia, or a parousia before the tribulation? I am not suggesting that tradition is always correct and has no error, but we need plain scripture to show that it is not that way. What scripture is it that clearly teaches that the Church and Israel do not exist together right up until Christ's parousia? There simply is none! That idea is supposition, conjecture, inference, and speculation. Eventually more modern Bibles will make the "restrainer" or "he that letteth" (II Thess. 2:7) the Holy Spirit, which is exactly what the New King James Bible did. The 1611 KJV says, *For the mystery of iniquity doth already work: only he who now letteth will let, until he be taken out of the way."* The NKJV ©1990 by Thomas Nelson says, *"For the mystery of lawlessness is already at work; only He who now restrains will do so until He is taken out of the way."* That, by the way, is the only version to my knowledge that has capitalized the word "he" thereby making "he" the Holy Spirit with no historical manuscript support or evidence whatsoever. Let us assume that was a mistake. And even though earlier MSS were in uncials (another fancy word for capital letters - 4th to the 8th century), still no later Latin or Greek MSS had interpreted the pronoun "he" to be the Holy Spirit; not even the false Catholic vulgate or the Greek modern texts capitalize that word. Since there over 225 "new and improved" translations, I would presume anyone can now re-write the Bible and introduce their own bias, or eliminate specific verses that are too offensive. Do they not play the role of the Holy Spirit? If Paul intended the restrainer to be the Holy Spirit, he simply would have said, "Only the Spirit who is now restraining, will restrain until He is taken out of the way." Let's face it, Paul uses the word "Spirit" in verse 13 of II Thessalonians 2, but clearly not in verse 7. It is all but certain that he didn't mean the Holy Spirit in this context.

Imminence and the Rapture

An imminent return of Christ, if taught to mean "any moment return," in scripture, it is not very apparent, at least not that I have found. So we need to address this subject. The proponents of a pre-trib rapture do not believe any signs are necessary before the coming (parousia) of Christ. If the scriptures teach imminency, then we are not to look at current world events, or things that have happened or are happening to Israel, nor are we to look for prophesied biblical events concerning the Jews. The belief in imminency demands that no relationship exist between current events and future Bible prophecy. Could Jesus have come back at any time in past history? – Yes! – Could that return have been imminent? – No! That's the difference between expectancy and imminency. All the necessary prophecies for Christ's parousia could have been fulfilled in any persons lifetime. The dictionary describes the word "imminent" as about to happen, or impending. How do the pre-trib believers know that Christ's return is just about to happen – they don't! – simple as that. His return hasn't happened, therefore the event could never have been imminent. The usage of the word is grammatically incorrect. A more fitting one is "expectancy." No matter what one's position of the coming of Christ and the accompanying resurrection is, we are all "expecting" it!

The fact that Israel has become a nation again in 1948 after 1900 years, and that Jews have re-gathered back into their homeland, would have no relation to prophecy if you hold to a pre-trib (pre-week rapture) position. The fact that Israel has regained the ownership of Jerusalem in 1967 would not have a bearing on His coming either. And if you acknowledge that the times are getting closer because of wicked activities in the world, then you have acknowledged signs. And by holding to the view that the church of the Laodoceans is the last church period, you cannot promote "any moment" imminency without impending signs.

But, we ought not abandon the usage of the word "imminence" just because the pre-tribbers think the parousia could happen at "any moment" without signs. I am truly expecting the 70th week to begin, based upon certain fulfilled prophecies, and thus the parousia would be imminent to me in that sense. It would fit Webster's definition of "impending" because Israel has now become a nation and Jerusalem has been re-captured. An example of what imminence is, is as follows: School always let's out sometime in the month of June; but just before that, there is always final exams. So you know when examination time arrives, then the time when school let's out is truly "imminent." To see a 7 year peace accord signed between Israel and many Arab nations, or the temple rebuilt, etc. would mean that the return of Christ is truly imminent.

In the past, if Israel was not a nation, and Jerusalem wasn't under their control, then the rapture or the day of the Lord could not have occurred at "any moment in time." It would certainly be difficult to support a scenario where the rapture took place, and the day of the Lord started, (God's wrath), but there was no nation, no temple, and no capital, which would thwart the armies of Antichrist from invading. All of these prophetic events constitute what Daniel called *"the time of the end"* (Dan. 12:4, 9). It would not have made much sense for Jesus to return before the Gospel was spread abroad, and before canon was completed (the canon codex of the Bible took about two more centuries to complete before we even had a complete Bible). Then there had to be a time period for the salvation of the Gentiles which Paul talked about, a time for the re-gathering of the Jews, and finally a time when they possessed Jerusalem. And there are still more signs to come. All of these things may have been accomplished in a persons lifetime from the time that they were born. That is still true today for any person born today – "expectancy," different from "imminence."

In the parable of the talents, Jesus said, *After a long time, the Lord of those servants cometh, and reckoneth with them"* (Mt. 25:19). This was a parable to the Jews about the second coming and the setting up of the kingdom. The implication was that there was going to be a lengthy time lapse between His death and His parousia. Then on another occasion when Jesus was praying to His Father, as recorded by John, He said, *"Neither pray I for those alone, but for them also which shall believe on me through their word..."* (Jn. 17:20). These were future souls that were to be saved! And again He said, in context, *I pray not that thou shouldest take them out of the world, but that thou shouldest keep them from the evil, as thou hast sent me into the world, even so have I sent them into the world"* (v.15, 18). Again, He sent them to witness to the future souls that were going to become Christians. I believe it would be reasonable to assume that Jesus was preparing them for a long lifetime battle and mission. We know this to be, because the conversion of Saul, the Pharisee, to Paul the Apostle, hadn't even occurred yet, and his mission was to spread the Gospel to the Gentiles. For Christ to return any sooner than the completion of these events would have vacated God's prophetic plan for Israel and the conversion of millions of Gentiles (like you and I).

Paul wrote, *"blindness in part is happened to Israel, until the fullness of the Gentiles comes in, and so all Israel shall be saved..."* (Ro. 11:25). It would seem implausible to think that the *"fullness of the Gentiles"* could have happened at "any moment." Also in Acts, Jesus said to His disciples, *"But ye shall receive power, after that the Holy Ghost is come upon you: and ye shall be witnesses unto me both in Judea, and Samaria, and unto the utter most part of the earth"* (Acts 1:8). This action certainly couldn't transpire in a moment of time; it would take many, many years, which history has shown. In just two verses before this one, a question was posed to Jesus, *"...Lord, wilt thou at this time restore again the kingdom to Israel?* (v. 6). His followers were looking for the immediate physical kingdom to be set up, and that's probably why they thought Jesus would return to the earth quickly after He left. There were a lot of things that they didn't understand, even though Jesus made it clear. His death and resurrection they couldn't understand, even after 3 years of traveling on the road with Him.

When Jesus was talking to Peter, He told him that he would

live to be an old man, and die by crucifixion in a manner that would glorify God. *"...but when thou shalt be old, thou shalt stretch forth thy hands, and another shall gird thee, and carry thee whither thou wouldest not. This spake He, signifying by what death he should glorify God..."* (Jn. 21:18-19). This passage unmistakably indicated that there would be many years before Peter would die by crucifixion as history has shown; but he lived many years after the death of Christ and thus became an old man. The return of Christ should, of necessity, have been viewed as "expectancy" not imminency (see glossary).

In the book of James, we read, *"Be ye also patient; stablish your hearts: for the coming* (parousia) *of the Lord draweth nigh"* (James 5:8). This verse is often used by pre-trib adherents to establish imminency, but as Peter also said, *But, beloved, be not ignorant of this one thing, that one day is with the Lord as a thousand years, and a thousand years as one day"* (II Pet. 3:8). So if the Lord's return was *"nigh"* (close), and He hasn't come back in almost two thousand years, then the event certainly wasn't imminent in the sense of "any moment." The closeness of the parousia, in retrospect of history, was that they were in the *"last days,"* (as we are today - Heb. 1:2) and have been since the death and resurrection of Jesus Christ. It was Calvary, that initiated God's timetable of the *"last days"* in which we live.

When examining some passages of scripture, there appears to be a long time period that must pass, before Christ returns which would seem to diminish the thought of an imminent parousia. For instance, when Peter was preaching to the Jews at Pentecost he said, *"[19]Repent, ye therefore, and be converted, that your sins may be blotted out when the times of refreshing shall come from the presence of the Lord; [20]and He shall send Jesus Christ, which before was preached unto you: [21]whom the heaven must receive until the times of restitution of all things,* *which God hath spoken by the mouth of all His holy prophets* *since the world began"* (Acts 3:19-21). Here we see that Jesus will remain in Heaven until the *"times of refreshing"* comes and the *"restitution of all things"* takes place. The pastors that I have spoken with, agree that those events will take place somewhere at the onset of the millennial kingdom. Our text says nothing about coming down 7 years or more earlier than the times of refreshing, or the time of restitution. To have the times of refreshing at the beginning of the week, would be indefensible when faced with such a plain passage of scripture.

When Jesus was talking to Ananias after Saul had received his call on the road to Damascus, He said, *"¹⁵Go thy way: for he* *is a chosen vessel unto me, to bear my name before the Gentiles,* *and kings, and the children of Israel: ¹⁶for I will shew him how* *great things he must suffer for my name's sake"* (Acts 9:15-16). Certainly, this charge of Christ to Paul could not have been accomplished in a "moment" of time, because it took Paul's entire lifetime to carry out this mission. Jesus could not be expected to return at "any moment." It should be considered here that "imminency" perhaps can be defined a little different then "any moment," and "without signs" in relation to the return of Christ. Maybe the parousia should be viewed with "expectancy," meaning that all necessary prophetic events before Christ's return could transpire in any persons lifetime. And now that Israel has re-gathered and Jerusalem again has become their capital city, as the prophets said, we can truly say that we are expecting the start of the 70ᵗʰ week in the near future, and perhaps within the lifetime of any person who is living today. There appears to be some confliction in the pre-tribulation thinking. Most pastors or laymen that I have met, who hold to

53

an "imminent" (any moment) return, cited two events that had to transpire before the rapture and the return of Christ:

1) The Jews had to have been re-gathered back into their land, as a nation, and

2) Jerusalem had to be under their control as the capital city.

And of course, that being the case, then how could Jesus have come back prior to 1948 unexpectedly? These are observable signs and would spoil the "any moment" theory. Hal Lindsey's stated, *"Another important event that had to take place* before *the stage would be fully set for the seven year countdown,* was the repossession of ancient Jerusalem.*" He then goes on to say, *"It is clear in these chapters that the Jews would have to be dwelling in and have possession of the ancient city of Jerusalem at the time of the Messiah's triumphant advent" (the "Late Great Planet Earth," 1970, Zondervan Pub. House p. 54).* On page 42 of the same book, he says, *"The general time of this seven-year period couldn't begin until the Jewish people re-established their nation in their ancient homeland of Palestine."* Mr. Lindsey seems to support an "any moment" rapture in his books, but then maintains there are signs before the 70th week can begin. Again, in the same book, and on page 57, he reasons, *"With the Jewish nation reborn in the land of Palestine, ancient Jerusalem once again under total Jewish control for the first time in 2600 years, and talk of rebuilding the great Temple, the most important prophetic sign of Jesus Christ's soon coming is before us. This has now set the stage for the other predicted signs to develop in history."* (he lists 20 other signs that has brought us closer to the rapture). Does he mean that at the time of the writing of his book, that the parousia was imminent, but not in past Church history?

Lindsey adheres to a silent, secret, rapture by stating, *"Jesus described the sudden parting of believers from unbelievers, when He comes <u>secretly</u> for His own. He said two men will be working in a field, one will be taken and the other left. Two women will be employed, side by side, and <u>one will suddenly disappear</u> and the other one will be left"* (Hal Lindsey, There's a New World Coming, Vision House Pub. 1973, p.81, 82). Accordingly, Christ comes in secret and no one sees Him but believers. One might ask where is it in scripture that alludes to this impression? Here, Lindsey is implying that the women who disappeared went to Heaven in the rapture. The problem with that thought is that it contradicts what Jesus said. When the Apostle asked where the woman would be taken, the reply of Jesus was, *"Wheresoever the body is, thither will the eagles* (vultures) *be gathered together"* (Lk. 17:37). The reply of Jesus certainly doesn't sound like she went up to Heaven, but rather to judgment, or a place of devastation like the battle in Megiddo. The prophet Joel said, *"²I will also gather <u>all nations</u>, and will bring them down into <u>the valley of Jehoshaphat</u>, and will plead with them there for my people and for my heritage Israel, whom they have scattered among the nations, and parted my land. ¹²Let the heathen be wakened, and come up to the valley of Jehoshaphat: for there will I sit to judge all the heathen round about"* (Joel 3:2, 12). This appears to be where the bodies of the wicked unbelievers will be dealt with when Christ returns for judgment and implements the battle of Armageddon. The description of the woman being removed, is a manifestation of the parable of the "wheat and the tares," with the tares (wicked) being removed first, and the leftovers (righteous Jews) will be permitted to enter into the kingdom.

Let's say for conversations sake, that a pre-trib parousia, in our scenario, transpires at the beginning of the week. Most pre-tribulationists agree that the Holy Spirit is removed from the scene when the Church is raptured (II Thess. 2:7). So, the Church is gone, Christians are raptured, and all of a sudden there is complete chaos over the entire planet. Millions of automobiles and planes crash, doctors, nurses and caregivers disappear, school age children never make it home, machinery of various sorts are left to themselves, Christian orphanages are left vacant, bankers, traders, investors can't be found, millions of people from all over the world suddenly vanish, and so on. What a picture! A silent, secret, no-sign rapture and resurrection. We are out of this sin sick world with no tribulation nor do we have a cross to carry in the tribulation. Now somehow, I don't think that these were the thoughts of the early Christians, but it would seem more fitting of a vision conjectured up in the early 19th century in England. I do admit that it is a very comforting thought for Christians, a "crown without a cross," and it most certainly preaches well in the churches tickling the ears of the weary saints, but is it really what the scriptures teach?

Now suddenly the ones who didn't get raptured and were "left behind," having heard the Gospel, will now want to become saved. So according to the pre-trib enthusiasts, there are millions and millions of people from all over the planet, who become Christians in the first half of the week after all of the Christians were raptured up to Heaven (they quote Rev. 7:9, who I believe are the numberless multitude of believers who endured the great tribulation and were raptured at His coming). But somehow these "second chance" souls become saved, even though the Holy Spirit isn't around to convict and indwell or empower them. This task is purportedly accomplished by the Jewish converts (the 144,000 - Rev. 7:4) who suddenly become world wide evangelists given supernatural powers like the prophets of the Old Testament. These 144,000 are the unsaved Jews, who were converted by the two witnesses in Revelation, chapter 11. Lindsey states, *"The Holy Spirit will endow the 144,000 chosen Israelites with the same kind of power He did the prophets in the Old Testament...but the unique Church economy ministries of indwelling, baptizing, sealing, gifting and filling of every believer* <u>*will be removed with the Church*</u>. *This is consistent with all that is revealed of the average Tribulational believer's level of spiritual insight, knowledge and maturity"* *(The Rapture, p.163)*. This theory creates another dilemma because pre-trib thinkers believe that the two witnesses begin their ministry at the beginning of the week and then are killed by Antichrist at the middle of the week. The problem with that thought is, John indicated that the two witnesses ascended up to Heaven after saying, *"The second woe is past; and behold the third woe* (the bowl/vial judgments) *cometh quickly..."* (Rev. 11:14). The second woe is the 6th trumpet. This clearly places us near the end of the trumpets, which according to <u>their</u> scenario ends in the middle of the week. That means the vials, which are contained in the 7th trumpet, would have to begin at the middle of the week, but considering what the 1st vial is, that would present another conflicting picture. The first vial is a punishment (past action) for those who took the mark and worshipped Antichrist or his image during the great tribulation. Antichrist, in the middle of the week, is arriving on the scene and is invading Jerusalem with his armies; this is the actual true "revealing" of him (Lk. 21:20).

Also, the idea that these newly converted Christians will not receive the Holy Spirit or His power, and are not part of the Church as defined by the Apostle Paul, is not fathomable to me. These new converts will now have to make it on their own power, and if they get martyred for the sake of Jesus Christ, they will never receive a glorified body, and will not reign with the other raptured saints, but will pro-create during the millennium producing offspring who rally against Jerusalem at the end of the 1000 years. With this scheme, pre-trib adherents may be introducing a new plan of salvation, and redemption. My opinion, for what its worth, is that this scenario is way off the map, out of the ballpark, and should be abandoned with a more realistic approach which is more in line with what scripture is really saying. There are too many problems with Christ coming at the start of the week, removing the Holy Spirit, and then having people getting saved in a different manner then what Paul taught. No scripture reveals another parousia prior to the time stated in Matthew 24:29-30. Jesus Christ will come once, and it will be after the great tribulation, at the end of the 70th week, and if anyone did become saved during the great tribulation, it will be because God called them through the Holy Spirit (which supposedly left).

Who Are the "Saints" in the Tribulation?

Another difficult concept for opponents of the pre-trib theory to comprehend, is that the saints in the New Testament are somehow different than the saints in the book of Revelation. And yet, adherents like Hal Lindsey give the proper definition of a "saint" by saying, *"The word 'saint' means someone who is set apart as Gods possession. It is used to designate all who have believed in Christ as Savior. This word is used many times to refer to those who will accompany Christ at His return." (the "Late Great Planet Earth" - 1970, Zondervan Pub. House p.173).* With that statement,

I certainly would agree! But then Lindsey goes back to the Old Testament where he refers to the return Christ with all of His saints at the <u>end</u> of the tribulation period. He quotes from Zechariah 14:5, *"...and the Lord my God, shall come, and <u>all the saints</u> with thee."* *(Late Great Planet Earth p. 173)*. How then, can the "saints" throughout the New Testament and specifically in the book of Revelation, not be part of the Church, and yet lay claim that the O.T. saints make up the Church? The martyred saints, (Rev. 20:4), who were beheaded for the witness of Jesus went through the great tribulation; are these not part of the Church? Jude 14 says, *"Behold, the Lord cometh with ten thousands of His saints."* The case for <u>not</u> identifying the saints in Revelation 6-19 as a part of the Church, is incredibly deficient! In many of the resurrection passages, as well as our rapture verses, the word "Church" is not mentioned either; but the exclusion does not mean that they are not the Church.

All pre-tribulationists agree with the Apostle Paul by describing the definition of the Church as a group of *"saints,"* but in the same breath they say that the *"saints"* in Revelation are not part of the Church, and are to be treated differently, and will not be afforded the sealing, gifts, or the indwelling of the Spirit? This I don't understand! There are many books in the New Testament pertaining to us as believers, but the word "church" is not mentioned one time. For instance: Jude, 1st and 2nd John, 2 Timothy, Titus, and 2nd Peter, etc. all omit the word "church." Does that mean we deem these books irrelevant to the applicability of Christian living just because the word "church" is missing, but contain the word saint? If you were to address a particular "Church" in a certain town, you would say, *"to the First Baptist <u>Church</u> in Marysville."* You wouldn't say, *"to all of the <u>saints</u> in Marysville,"* because there may be many more saints in Marysville that in that particular church. And that's the way it is in the book of Revelation; Jesus addresses a particular Church with a particular name, like the Church of Philadelphia; afterwards John is talking about the saints throughout the book, who make up the universal Church and who are in the future tribulation: the body of Christ. We see the Church in full view, all throughout Revelation; especially in chapters 6-19 – they are the saints who resisted the mark, and will be resurrected or raptured as Christ returns to the Mount of Olives. They also will receive glorified bodies as part of the Church (Ro. 8:28-30).

The Elect of God

The question of who the "elect" are in Matthew 24, is a much debated one, and if the "elect" are all saved Jews and Gentiles, then there is no debate as to when the rapture would be. It would be post-tribulational because Jesus declares, *"²⁹Imme-diately after the tribulation of those days, shall the sun be darkened, and the moon shall not give her light, and the stars shall fall from heaven, and the powers of the heavens shall be shaken...³⁰and they shall see the Son of man coming in the clouds of heaven with power and great glory. ³¹And He shall send His angels with a great sound of a trumpet, and they shall gather together His elect from the four winds, from one end of heaven to the other"* (vs. 29-31 which is a consistent description of the rapture event). To view all of the *"elect"* in the New Testament as a part of the *"Church,"* is proper and consistent with scripture.

In Matthew 24, the pre-trib thinkers do the same thing with the term *elect* as they do with the term *saints* in the book of Revelation. The saints are always the *"elect"* in the N.T. but not in Matthew 24, and then they say that the *"saints"* are not the Church all the time. The pre-tribbers are not consistent with their methods of interpretation and consequently arrive at an unnatural distorted view of the end times. Their view, no matter how popular, is a recent departure from the normal historical view. We are God's saints and we are His elect! Proper exegesis (another scholarly word meaning explaining, or critical interpreting) is the foundation of Bible theology. It demands the analysis of scripture using literal, grammatical and historical methodology. We need to view the text in its normal meaning of the language, and use grammatical rules properly, and then look at the passage from a historical, political, and cultural view of the times in which it was written. This would be a beginning to properly understand the text. We must be hermeneutically (one of them fancy terms again, simply meaning to interpret or explain things) exacting, especially in the book of Matthew. I will attempt to give you my thoughts and scriptural evidence to demonstrate that the message that Jesus was delivering, was not just for the Jews, but for the elected Church as well, and when Jesus used the word *"elect"* it was for all believers who follow Him.

In the "Olivet Discourse," (Matthew 24), Jesus is speaking to His disciples who are following Him. He is not addressing the *"multitude"* of Jews whom He spoke to in parables, nor is He addressing the Pharisees and other Jews who were in the temple as in the chapter before. These Apostles knew the interpretation of all of the previous parables that Jesus had taught about future things. They knew of the wheat and the tares; (Mt. 13); they also knew that they would be reigning over future Israel in the millennial kingdom (Mt. 19:28); they knew that Jesus was coming with His angels and administrating rewards to the saints (Mt. 16:27). Peter, who walked on water, knew what glorified bodies looked like (Mt. 17:1-3). These Apostles knew that He was the Christ, their Messiah, and indeed, God manifested in the flesh. They were of the *"elect."* They are a part of the future Church and we find that everything Jesus told them in this discourse, was in harmony with the same *"coming"* that He told them about in Mt. 16:27. Since we know that the Apostles were a part of the Church, why would Jesus be telling them things that would only relate to the Jews and not to the future of the Church as well? The question of the Apostles, was, *"What will be the sign of thy coming and of the end of the world?"* (Mt. 24:3). The majority of the Jews were blinded to the teachings of Christ and of the New Testament Church, so the answer was given to His chosen believers. He chose not to reveal the true meaning of the parables to the multitude because of their hardened hearts (Mt. 13:10-15). It is interesting to note that Dr. Walvoord argued that the Church is missing from the discourse because the disciples were asking about the coming of the millennial kingdom; and therefore has no relevance to the Church *(Blessed Hope, p.86-87)*, but that statement appears to be misleading. In the parallel passages in Mark and Luke, the same question was asked about the temple, and in Matthew, the question was asked His parousia and the consummation of the age and there is no mention of any question regarding the kingdom. It is hard to believe that the consummation of the age and the parousia of Christ would not be relevant to the Church; especially when Jesus said that He would be with the Church until the end of the world (Mt. 28:20).

We know that all of end time prophecy is Jewish, so naturally everything will relate to the Jews because that's who Christ was relating to in prophecy; but that has nothing to do with the presence of the Church during the past 2,000 years of history and our parallel existence with Israel. We will be together with them, and they with us, until all prophecy has been fulfilled pertaining to Israel right up until the time that they become saved. Paul tells us that, *"²⁵For I would not, brethren, that ye should be ignorant of this mystery, lest ye should be wise in you own conceits; that blindness in part is happened to Israel, until the fullness of the Gentiles be come in. ²⁶And so all Israel shall be saved: as it is written, there shall come out of Zion the Deliverer and shall turn away ungodliness from Jacob: ²⁷for this is my covenant with them, when I shall take away their sins"* (Ro. 11:25-27). Paul is saying that the fullness of the Gentiles is not until the <u>end</u> of the 70ᵗʰ week, and then the *"Deliverer"* will come and take away all of their sins; this is the fulfillment of Daniel's 70 weeks of prophecy (9:24). So the Church is still around until the *"Deliverer"* comes, and Israel's sins are removed, which occurs at the end of the week, and most certainly, not at the beginning (Dan. 9:24).

Paul calls both the saints and the Church, the "elect." In Romans he wrote, *"He that spared not his own Son, but delivered him up <u>for us all</u>, how shall he not with him also freely give us all things? Who shall lay any thing to the charge of <u>God's elect</u>? It is God that justifieth"* (8:32-33). Here the *"elect"* are Christians who comprise the Church.

And then in Colossians, Paul says, *"Where there is neither Greek nor Jew, circumcision nor uncircumcision, Barbarian, Scythian, bond nor free: but Christ is all, and in all. Put on therefore, as <u>the elect of God</u>...*(3:11-12). All who believe are of the elect and are called the *"elect."* Here Paul is including the Gentiles and the Jews.

Paul writing to Titus in the third person declares, *"Paul, a*

63

servant of God, and an apostle of Jesus Christ, according to the faith of God's <u>elect</u>...(1:1). He calls Titus, *"mine own son after the common faith."* Again, the Church consistently continues to be the *"elect"* in scripture.

Peter addressing the Church, penned, *"<u>Elect</u> according to the foreknowledge of God the Father, through sanctification of the Spirit...who are kept by the power of God through faith unto salvation <u>ready to be revealed in the last time</u>"* (I Pet. 1:1,5). The revealing is at the end of the week which is the same as the appearing and the coming.

There are several more passages that consistently support the fact that the *"elect"* and the "Church" are interchangeable in the New Testament. If you chose not to find the "Church" in the book of Matthew, then the great commission in Chapter 28 would not have relevance to the Church. To say that the elect in Matthew 24, are someone else, other than Jews and saved Gentiles, would require New Testament proof to the contrary, and that is lacking in the pre-trib theory. And if you decide to make the *"elect"* only Jews in Mt. 24, you are really saying that the parousia, in the context of Matthew 24, is for the Jews only; and that would be contrary to other scripture. Again, the evidence points to a single parousia, where the angels are gathering together the "Church," which Jesus says is post-trib. He comes: (a) with a shout, (b) at the last trumpet, (c) with the voice of the archangel, (d) with His holy angels and saints, and (e) every eye shall see Christ in His glory. John tells us that many people of the earth shall wail because they knew that they were wrong, including Israel (Rev. 1:7); and when He does come, it indeed will not be secret or silent. This time He returns suddenly with judgment, and not as the baby in the manger, but as King of Kings and Lord of Lords (Rev. 19:16), to rule over the earth with a rod of iron.

Revelation 3:10 and the Rapture

Before we leave the subject of the rapture, let's discuss one of the "proof" texts of the pre-trib theory which is used to remove the Church from the tribulation; it is Revelation 3:10. This verse, in context, is directed to the Church of Philadelphia, the church dubbed, the "missionary church" by most dispensationalists. The verse says, *"Because thou hast kept the word of my patience, I also will keep thee from the hour of temptation, which shall come upon all the world, to try them that dwell upon the earth."* The controversy in this verse is the phrase, *"keep thee from."* We find that the church of Philadelphia and the church of Smyrna (Rev. 2:8), were the only two churches of the seven that Jesus had no rebuke regarding their conduct. I certainly don't think that could be said of the Western churches today, and especially here in the United States. The description of our conduct would be more like the church of Laodocia (Rev. 3:14-17).

Jesus said to the Smyrna church, *"Fear none of those things which thou shalt suffer: behold, the devil shall cast some of you into prison, that ye may be tried; and ye shall have tribulation ten days: be thou faithful unto death, and I will give thee a crown of life."* (Rev. 2:10). From this text, I certainly don't see any special deliverance for these guys; they were in tribulation and some, or all, appeared to have been killed. These saints were faithful and obedient to the Gospel, but yet suffered tribulation and perhaps even death because of their convictions. So what makes us think that we, as part of the Church, are so special that we deserve to be spared from the testing of our faith when the trial comes upon us? We are spared from the intense wrath of God (the day of the Lord), but not from the final wrath of Satan who will muster up all of his rage in his last days. Nowhere in God's word does He exempt the saints from tribulation, and the Bible is replete with many examples of how we will suffer in this world right up until the last of the week. God receives the glory when we suffer for Him. John said of the Christians in the great tribulation, *"¹²Here is the patience of the saints: here are they that keep the commandments of God, and the faith of Jesus. ¹³And I heard a voice from heaven saying unto me, Write, <u>Blessed are the dead which die in the Lord from henceforth:</u> Yea, saith the Spirit, that they may rest from their labors; and their works do follow them"* (Rev. 15:12-13).

The church that is being addressed in our 3:10 text is Philadelphia. They had no rebuke; they were the model church. But like I said, isn't the Western Church today more like the historical church of Laodocia? That church was lukewarm, lackadaisical, materialistic, selfish and certainly lacking the first love of Christ. They thought they were ok with their performance, but Christ said to them, *"¹⁵I know thy works, that thou art neither cold nor hot: I would thou wert cold or hot. ¹⁶So then because thou art lukewarm, and neither cold nor hot, I will spue thee out of my mouth. ¹⁷Because thou sayest, I am rich, and increased with goods, and have need of nothing; and knowest not that thou art wretched, and miserable, and poor, and blind, and naked:"* (Rev. 3:15-17). Why should we be whisked away when we have dirty robes that need cleaning from the sin of this world? Did not the Church suffer incredible persecution under Nero? How about the Popes and all of their torture devices used during the inquisition upon the Christians? All throughout history, including today, Christians have been tortured and persecuted. The world has always been against God's people because we are His ambassadors; they hated Jesus Christ, and they hate us because we are His followers, or at least supposed to be. The Word teaches that the believer will suffer persecution right up until the time He comes back, and who would know more about that than the believers at the hands of the Roman Church during the inquisition, and the Christians under the Roman Emperors.

The portion of Rev. 3:10, which states, *"I also will keep thee from the hour of temptation"* is one that has been much debated with the same old arguments. One side says it means to remove from the tribulation, and the other side says it means to protect or guard while in the midst of tribulation. In the process of the debate, the Greek scholars bring out the Greek words *"tereo"* (tay-reh'-o - keep) and *"ek"* (ek - from), and proceed with a prolific volume of information on those two words and their exact meaning. (not knowing Greek like the scholars, you will be blessed by being spared from the agony of their discourse on those two words) The only other place those exact expressions *"keep"* and *"from"* are used, is in John 17:15. In that passage, Jesus is praying to the Father on behalf of His disciples and says, *"I have given them thy word; and the world hath hated them, because they are not of the world, even as I am not of the world. I pray not that thou shouldest take them out of the world, but that thou shouldest keep them from the evil."* Certainly we see here that *"keep"* and *"from"* gives the impression of guarding or protecting and not the removal from the world. Jesus prayed to give them safe passage through the world of tribulation, protecting their souls, but not necessarily their physical bodies. This keeping within the sphere of trouble brings God the glory, which He wouldn't receive if the Church was removed out of it. To be removed totally from tribulation would seem to be contrary to what John said. He had a vision of a numberless multitude of believers from every nation, tribe, kindred and language, who went through the great tribulation. When John asked the angel who all this countless multitude was, the angel told him, "...*These are they which came out of great tribulation, and have washed their robes, and made them white in the blood of the Lamb*" (Rev. 7:14). These saints (and they were not second rate Christians who will not be glorified) went through the great tribulation and are now raptured before the throne of God. They were <u>not</u> removed from it, but were kept from taking the mark or worshipping Antichrist to the saving of their souls. We know that no saint will take the mark or worship the beast! (Rev 13:8). Perhaps if we all interpret the phrase, "*I will keep thee from the hour of temptation...,*" as the protection from the "*day of the Lord,*" then all positions could be accommodated. The question would then be, when does that day <u>start</u>?

Most dispensationalists, and godly men like C.I. Scofield, Gary Cohen, Salem Kirban, assert that the 7 churches in Asia are representative or typify Church history. Most assign arbitrary dates for the opening and closing of each historical period, declaring that the church of Laodocia, the 7ᵗʰ Asian church, is the final period of time before the return of Christ. Philadelphia, for example, was the missionary and revival period (A.D. 1750-1900 – depending on who made up the dating). This they do this without any scriptural backing whatsoever. Who determines these dates? Who declares they are periods of history? Where is the exegetical proof! When you take the special message given by Jesus to the church of Philadelphia, and then apply it to <u>all</u> believers 2000 years in the future, it makes that special message meaningless to that particular church. The saints in Philadelphia were given that promise based upon their past behavior and it was not meant for all Christendom. As dispensationalists, let us be careful not to spiritualize scripture the way we accuse the amillennialists or the post-millennialists of doing. Maybe it would be more reasonable to view these 7 churches as types of churches as well as physical ones, which were in Asia started by the Apostle Paul.

One final thought about the Revelation 3:10 text; if this verse is supposed to be dealing with the rapture, then why is it in the 6th period and not the 7th which is supposed to be the last period of history? It would seem that we should find the rapture text in the Church of Laodocia. All of the 7 literal churches that Jesus was rebuking and commending are, in my opinion, are representing types of churches in the last days, instead of historical time periods. And besides, there is nothing said in the Bible about a "Church age" that segregates the Church from the 70th week which is truly the last week in mans history; this age (really the age of grace if we must name it, but no matter what it is called, it must include the final week) ends at the conclusion of the 70th week just like Daniel said (Dan. 9:24). The 70 weeks (490 years) are over when the sins of Israel are forgiven, everlasting righteousness prevails for all believers, and the recognition of Christ as King of kings, and Lord of lords.

So, to sum up Revelation 3:10, the verse will always be debated because there is no agreement on when the rapture or the day of the Lord is. However, it appears that we are all in agreement in believing that the phrase, *"I also will keep thee from the hour of temptation, which shall come upon all the world,"* is really a reference to the *"day of the Lord,"* even though we don't think of it that way. We are all in agreement, but don't even realize it – that's funny! The pre-tribbers say that the phrase means the removal of the Church from the entire 70th week, which they call the <u>day of the Lord</u>. The pre-wrath people also exempts the Church from the <u>day of the Lord,</u> which they believe starts at the 7th seal, after the rapture. And finally, the post-tribbers also see the rapture and removal of the Church before the <u>day of the Lord</u> which they see as beginning at the end of the week. So we all agree that the Church is spared the *"day of the Lord"* and must conclude that the phrase, *"hour of temptation"* is the day of the Lord. So it all goes back as to when the day starts.

Revelation 4:1 - ("Come up hither...")

This is a text that was widely used to indicate that the Church was raptured into Heaven before the week started, but is not used very much anymore for obvious reasons. Our text says, *"¹After this I looked, and, behold, a door was opened in heaven: and the first voice which I heard was as it were of a trumpet talking with me; which said, <u>Come up hither,</u> and I will show thee things which must be hereafter. ²And immediately I was in the spirit; and, behold, a throne was set in heaven, and one sat on the throne"* (Rev. 4:1-2). In context, John was having a visionary experience to be shown the things that were going to occur in the future, that is, future to him. In other chapters John is back down on earth (e.g. Rev. 13:1); but if the call to Heaven was meant to be the Church, then does that mean the Church goes up and then comes down and then goes back up and then comes back down? I don't think so! Walvoord, in his book, *"Revelation,"* p.103, correctly says, *"There is no authority for connecting the rapture with this expression."* Not much more needs to be said on this text.

The Apostasy ("Falling away" – II Thessalonians 2:1-8)

In chapter two of II Thessalonians, Paul is reminding the troubled saints that the day of the Lord hadn't come yet. The church of Thessalonica was a young church and was not yet mature enough to grasp all of the radical truth that Paul taught. In addition, there were false letters in circulation, supposedly from Paul, which said the day of the Lord (day of Christ) was upon them. He corrects that notion and tells them that there would be a falling away (a defection or abandonment) from the faith first, and that Antichrist would show himself sitting in the temple as God before that day occurred. Then he goes on to talk about the restrainer being taken out of the way. Our complete text says, *"¹Now we beseech you* (beg you earnestly), *brethren, by the coming* (parousia) *of our Lord Jesus Christ, and by our gathering together unto him* (rapture), *²that ye be not soon shaken in mind, or be troubled, neither by spirit, nor by word, nor by letter as from us, as that the <u>day of Christ</u>* (day of the Lord) *is at hand. ³Let no man deceive you by any means: for that day* (day of the Lord) *shall not come, except there come <u>a falling away first, and that man of sin be revealed,</u>* (Antichrist) *the son of perdition; ⁴who opposeth and exalteth himself above all that is called God, or that is worshipped; so that he as God sitteth in the temple of God, showing himself that he is God. ⁵Remember ye not, that, when I was yet with you, I told you these things? ⁶And now ye know what withholdeth that he might be revealed in his time. ⁷For the mystery of iniquity doth already work: <u>only he who now letteth will let, until he be taken out of the way.</u> ⁸And then shall that Wicked be revealed, whom the Lord shall consume with the spirit of his mouth, and shall destroy with the brightness of his coming* (parousia):

71

⁸Even him, whose coming is after the working of Satan..." (II Thess. 2:1-8). In the above passage, we can summarize:

1) The saints thought the day of the Lord was upon them and that they had missed the rapture.

2) There would be a falling away (apostasy) before the day of the Lord came.

3) The man of sin (Antichrist) would be revealed before the day of the Lord.

4) Christ would destroy the man of sin (Antichrist) at His coming (parousia).

Paul made it clear to them, that the apostasy or *"falling away"* had to come <u>before</u> the day of the Lord (apostasy is the abandonment of what one has professed). In today's theological circles, there is a difference of opinion as to the meaning of the predicted apostasy. Some would say (like Marvin Rosenthal in his *"Pre-wrath Rapture of the Church,"* 1990) that it is a total <u>abandonment of the Jewish faith</u>, which would occur at the beginning of the week when the peace accord is signed between the many citizens of Israel and Antichrist. His supporting text is Isaiah 28:15,18, *"¹⁵Because ye have said, We have made a <u>covenant with death</u>, and with hell are we at agreement; when the overflowing scourge shall pass through, it shall not come unto us: for we have made lies our refuge, and under falsehood have we hid ourselves...¹⁸And your covenant with death shall be disannulled, and your agreement with hell shall not stand; when <u>the overflowing scourge</u> shall pass through, then ye shall be trodden down by it."* The "overflowing scourge" would be the time of Jacob's trouble (Jer. 30:7; the great tribulation, to which we all agree, begins at the middle of the week). This appears to have sound merit based upon scripture and perhaps is better than pure conjecture.

This would be similar to what happened when Antiochus Epiphanes IV, king of Syria (155-163 B.C. a type of Antichrist), made decrees that caused many Jews to embrace the Greek culture and worship the many Greek gods. It was through bribery, the high priest of Jerusalem turned to those Greek gods, adopted their culture, and profaned the Jewish temple. Eventually, when the godly Jews wouldn't bend and bow (although history tells us that many did), Jerusalem was invaded and destroyed by an army of over 22,000 Syrians. They raped the women, pillaged the temple, and slaughtered many godly Jews. History records that over 10,000 went into captivity at that time. This was the time when the human-like form of Zeus Olympus was set up and a pig roasted on the alter in the temple. It was about 5 years later, that a Jewish rebellion against the Syrians occurred, which historically is called, the "Maccabean Revolt." The coming Antichrist, much more wicked and powerful than Antiochus Epiphanes IV, will accomplish a similar deed, and with the full power of Satan. As a side note, this was the general time period when the false writings of the Apocrypha came into being, that are currently used in the Catholic Church today.

Another school of thought about the *"falling away,"* is when the so called "Christians" totally abandon their faith in God. The parenthesis around "Christians" is because there are millions today that profess to believe in God, who are not actually of the "elect" and not saved. They go to liberal apostate churches, they sit on a padded pew, sing the praise songs, drop a dollar bill in the offering plate, help in the soup lines, socialize, participate in pot-lucks, and seemingly in every way mimic the true believers, but really know not God or the power of the Holy Spirit. These are the ones that Paul cautions Timothy about what would happen in the last days, when he said, *"¹Now the Spirit speaketh expressly, that in the latter times some shall depart from the faith, giving heed to seducing spirits, and doctrines of devils; ...¹⁵Having a form of godliness, but denying the power thereof: from such turn away"* (I Tim. 4:1; II Tim. 3:15). And Paul said to Timothy, *"³For the time will come when they will not endure sound doctrine; but after their own lusts shall they heap to themselves teachers, having itching ears; ⁴And they shall turn away their ears from the truth, and shall be turned unto fables"* (II Tim. 4:3-4). Next we have John exhorting the saints, *"They went out from us, but they were not of us; for if they had been of us, they would no doubt have continued with us: but they went out, that they might be made manifest that they were not all of us"* (I John 2:19). And finally, Paul tells them that God will send them a strong delusion that they will believe a lie, *"¹⁰And with all deceivableness of unrighteousness in them that perish; because they received not the love of the truth, that they might be saved. ¹¹And for this cause God shall send them strong delusion, that they should believe a lie..."* (II Thess. 2:10-11).

Whatever your viewpoint of the two interpretations may be, the fact still remains that the *"falling away"* (apostasy) occurs before the day of the Lord. Since John and Paul were addressing the Church, of Thessalonica, I should think that the apostasy relates to "professing Christians." In addition, Paul also makes another dogmatic statement, declaring that the *"man of sin"* (Antichrist) would also be revealed (to the Jews and other believers), prior to the day of the Lord. So, we have two definite "signs" that will precede the day of the Lord. It was also scripturally established in previous discussion, that the *"day of the Lord"* would commence sometime <u>after</u> the cosmic events, and immediately <u>after</u> the parousia (appearing) of Christ; which all happens immediately <u>after</u> the great tribulation; therefore, it appears that if all of these events occurred at the start of the week (or several weeks prior as Hal Lindsey suggests), their placement would seem to be greatly distorted.

The Restrainer (II Thessalonians 2:6-8)

There is also a diversity of opinion who or what the "restrainer" is. Paul taught them, saying, *"⁶And now ye know what* (Grk. neuter gender) *withholdeth that he* (Grk. masculine) *might be revealed in his time. ⁷For the mystery* (concealing, or covering up) *of iniquity doth already work: <u>only he who now letteth will let,</u>* (restrains, hinders) *<u>until he be taken out of the way.</u> ⁸And <u>then</u> shall that Wicked* (Antichrist) *be revealed..."* Our Greek word for *"letteth"* is "katecho" (kat-ekh'-o), and has several English translations, and its primary meaning gives the sense of impeding, restraining, or hindering. There is also a translation of "allowing" which is the common meaning in its English usage today (e.g. "I will <u>let</u> [or allow] Jim go to the game with his friends.") Paul insinuated that there was someone or something that was "restraining," or "hindering" the man of sin from being revealed too early. And this personage was also present as Paul was talking to the brethren. So, if this personage was present then, and will be present in the future, it certainly couldn't be an ordinary man; therefore it must be either the Holy Spirit, an angelic being, or a succession of governments. We shall examine those thoughts in a moment.

Paul also is saying that the "mystery of iniquity" is <u>already</u>

at work, but apparently it has not yet developed into the intense, demonic sinful state of affairs that will occur when the man of sin is fully revealed. This *"mystery of iniquity"* actually was the "behind the scenes" working of Satan trying to distort the Gospel truth and to corrupt the message that God had given to the Paul and the Apostles. Satan couldn't corrupt Jesus by temptation, but he surely could deceive and take control of sinful men; which is exactly what he did. John had sternly warned believers that anyone who denied that Jesus was the Messiah and that Christ did not come in the flesh, was a liar and an antichrist. John also said, *"'Beloved, believe not every spirit, but try the spirits whether they are of God: because many false prophets are gone out into the world...³And every spirit that confesseth not that Jesus Christ is come in the flesh is not of God: and this is that spirit of antichrist, whereof ye have heard that it should come; and even now already is it in the world"* (I John 4:1, 3). And Jude cautioned them also by saying, *"For there are certain men crept in unawares, who were before of old ordained to this condemnation, ungodly men, turning the grace of our God into lasciviousness, and denying the only Lord God, and our Lord Jesus Christ"* (Jude 1, 4). This was the time period (and for the next 400 years) when Gnosticism (mixture of Greek and Oriental philosophy with a little Christianity), Modalism (denial of Trinity), Adoptionism (denied Jesus was deity at birth, but when God put Him through the test, He was adopted into the Godhead), Arianism (Jesus was a created being, but not equal with God), Mithraism (astrology and fertility worship, subterranean temples), Docetism (Christ only appeared to be human because He suffered and was tempted, therefore He couldn't be a deity), and all of other "ism's" abounded, and were distorting or denying the deity of Jesus Christ, which was the real issue and still is today.

Now, regarding the "restrainer," there was various interpretations throughout Church history as to who the restrainer was. Today, with almost 2000 years behind us, we can certainly see who it wasn't. Traditionally, down through Church history, the restrainer was thought to be human government and their laws, acting as a brake to prevent evil from overrunning society. For instance, the Roman government (after Constantine converted to Christianity in 331 A.D.), and all succeeding governments thereafter, were thought to be the ones that restrained the "man of sin" from coming upon the scene before his appointed time. This was accomplished through civil laws and their enforcement, but civil government cannot be a "he" and does not fit the masculine singular, nor do governments deal with actions on a spiritual level as required in our text under consideration. Whoever the restrainer is, he was existing during Paul's time and has been for the past 2000 years and can work on a spiritual plane.

More recently, and because of the development of pre-tribulational dispensationalism (in relation to eschatology, meaning, – a total separation of Israel from the Church, to the extent that the Church cannot even be around when Jewish prophecy is being fulfilled), the *"restrainer"* is believed to be the <u>Holy Spirit</u>. This identification, however, is rejected by most mid-tribulationalists, pre-wrathers, and post-tribulationalists. By making the "he" the Holy Spirit and then removing Him at the beginning of the week, presents several problems. (Text continues on page 92.)

I list five thoughts and difficulties by removing the Holy Spirit at the beginning of the week:

1) First, there is no direct evidence that the Holy Spirit is the restrainer. Paul simply does not say who he is. It is pure supposition to dogmatically teach that the Holy Spirit is the restrainer who holds back the revealing of Antichrist without scripture to support such a claim. Who the *"he"* is, is an educated guess at best (to accommodate a pre-tribulation bias, the NKJV makes the *"he,"* in II Thess. 2:7, the Holy Spirit by capitalizing *"he"* without supporting textual foundation).

2) If the Holy Spirit works through the Church (who are individuals), and the Church is removed before the week, then how do the millions of Christians receive Christ during the tribulation? To suggest that the Holy Spirit somehow operates differently (by not indwelling, or sealing them) during that time period, is not supported by any scripture. Paul plainly stated that the Holy Spirit indwells every Christian without exception, he affirms, *"⁴There is one body, and <u>one Spirit</u>, even as ye are called in one hope of your calling; ⁵One Lord, one faith, one baptism, ⁶One God and Father of all, who is above all, and through all, and <u>in you all</u>"* (Eph. 4:4-6 and others). The Holy Spirit does not come "on us" but dwells "in us." However, not all would agree with the Apostle Paul! Some put forward the idea that the method of salvation regresses back to the Old Testament way without the indwelling, sealing, gifting, or comforting of the Holy Spirit. That idea seems to be a pre-tribulational design to support the idea of the Church being removed before the week begins.

3) According to the pre-trib theory, the 144,000 Jewish witnesses supernaturally convert the great *"numberless multitude which no man could number"* (Rev. 7:9) to Christ. How can this be accomplished without the presence and indwelling of the Holy Spirit? If believers today, and in the past haven't accomplished this task in 2000 years <u>with</u> the presence of the Holy Spirit, then how could these Jews do it in a 42 month time frame <u>without</u> Him? Where will the conviction of sin come from to establish the need for repentance to salvation; especially with the operation and wicked influence of Antichrist and the false prophet? When Jesus Himself was here on earth and performing miracles there were still those who refused to believe on Him. Paul said, *"...¹⁰And with all deceivableness of unrighteousness in them that perish; because they received not the love of the truth, that they might be saved. ¹¹And for this cause <u>God shall send them strong delusion</u>, that they should believe a lie..."* (II Thess. 2:10-11). But Jesus said He will be with all believers until the very end, *"Teaching them to observe all things whatsoever I have commanded you: and, lo, I am with you always, even <u>unto the end of the world</u>"* (Mt. 28:20). It would certainly seem difficult to read into the statement that Jesus made, the idea that the end of the world (age) comes before the 70th week begins. Jesus never mentioned or taught of a specific time period that the pre-trib people call the "Church age;" but rather *"the end of the world,"* or the conclusion of all human activity prior to His parousia. The age that Jesus taught is the same age that we now live in, and will end when man is no longer in control. After this age, Christ will take back the title deed of the earth and run things the way that He originally intended,

Chart 1: Millennial and 2nd Advent (Parousia) Views

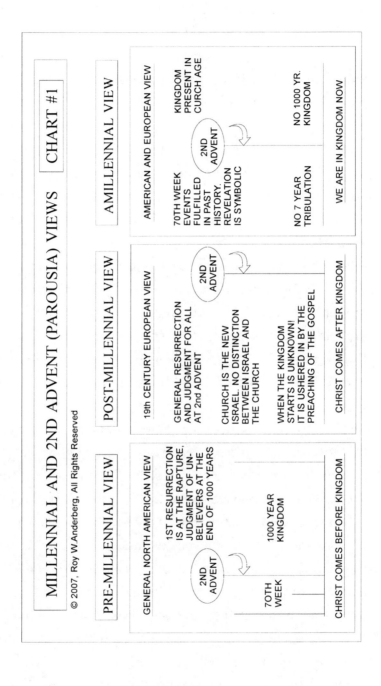

MILLENNIAL AND 2ND ADVENT (PAROUSIA) VIEWS   CHART #1

© 2007, Roy W.Anderberg, All Rights Reserved

AMILLENNIAL VIEW

AMERICAN AND EUROPEAN VIEW

70TH WEEK EVENTS FULFILLED IN PAST HISTORY. REVELATION IS SYMBOLIC

2ND ADVENT

KINGDOM PRESENT IN CURCH AGE

NO 7 YEAR TRIBULATION

NO 1000 YR. KINGDOM

WE ARE IN KINGDOM NOW

POST-MILLENNIAL VIEW

19th CENTURY EUROPEAN VIEW

GENERAL RESURRECTION AND JUDGMENT FOR ALL AT 2nd ADVENT

CHURCH IS THE NEW ISRAEL. NO DISTINCTION BETWEEN ISRAEL AND THE CHURCH

WHEN THE KINGDOM STARTS IS UNKNOWN! IT IS USHERED IN BY THE PREACHING OF THE GOSPEL

2ND ADVENT

CHRIST COMES AFTER KINGDOM

PRE-MILLENNIAL VIEW

GENERAL NORTH AMERICAN VIEW

1ST RESURRECTION IS AT THE RAPTURE. JUDGMENT OF UN-BELIEVERS AT THE END OF 1000 YEARS

2ND ADVENT

70TH WEEK

1000 YEAR KINGDOM

CHRIST COMES BEFORE KINGDOM

80

Chart 2: Rapture Locations

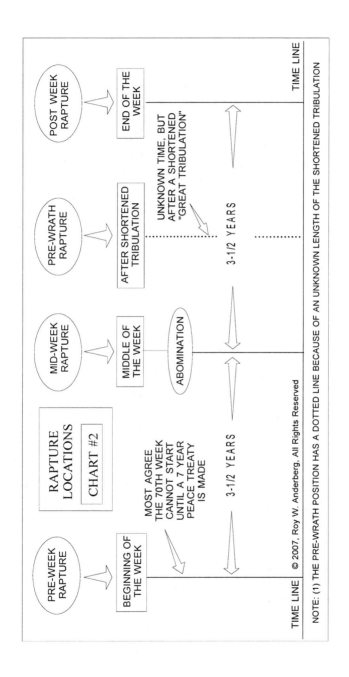

Chart 3: 2nd Advent of Jesus Christ

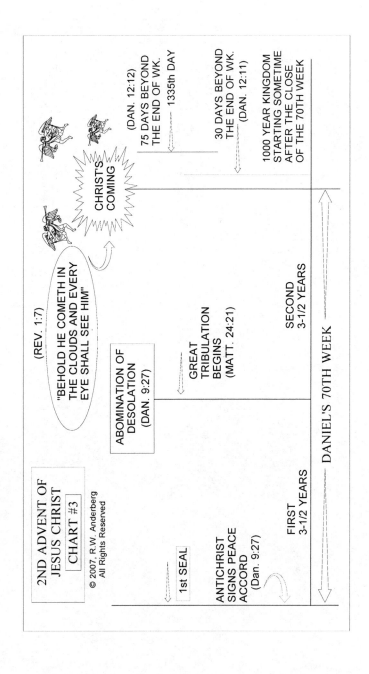

82

Chart 4: General Location of Pre-tribulation Events

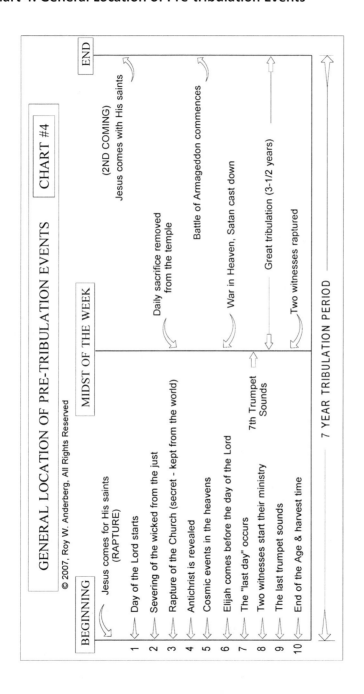

GENERAL LOCATION OF PRE-TRIBULATION EVENTS — CHART #4

BEGINNING — MIDST OF THE WEEK — END

Jesus comes for His saints (RAPTURE)

(2ND COMING) Jesus comes with His saints

1. Day of the Lord starts
2. Severing of the wicked from the just
3. Rapture of the Church (secret - kept from the world)
4. Antichrist is revealed
5. Cosmic events in the heavens
6. Elijah comes before the day of the Lord
7. The "last day" occurs
8. Two witnesses start their ministry
9. The last trumpet sounds
10. End of the Age & harvest time

7th Trumpet Sounds

Daily sacrifice removed from the temple

Battle of Armageddon commences

War in Heaven, Satan cast down

Great tribulation (3-1/2 years)

Two witnesses raptured

7 YEAR TRIBULATION PERIOD

Chart 5: Pre-tribulation Model

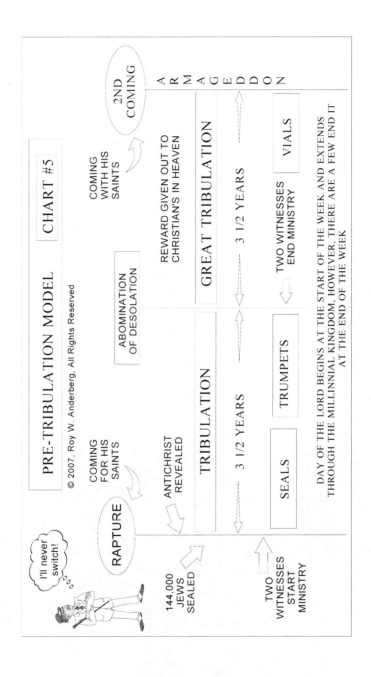

Chart 6: Pre-wrath Rapture Model

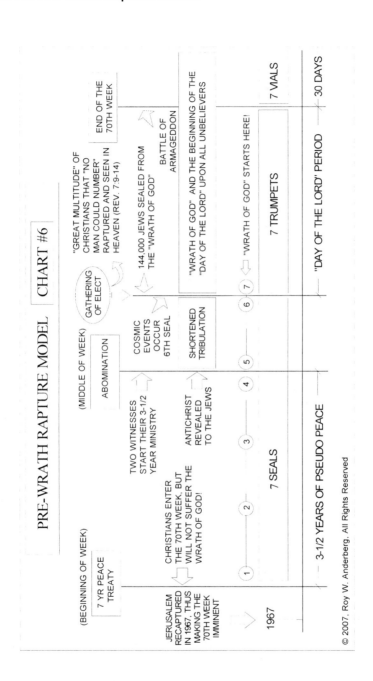

PRE-WRATH RAPTURE MODEL | CHART #6

(BEGINNING OF WEEK)

7 YR PEACE TREATY

JERUSALEM RECAPTURED IN 1967, THUS MAKING THE 70TH WEEK IMMINENT

1967

3-1/2 YEARS OF PSEUDO PEACE

7 SEALS

CHRISTIANS ENTER THE 70TH WEEK, BUT WILL NOT SUFFER THE WRATH OF GOD!

TWO WITNESSES START THEIR 3-1/2 YEAR MINISTRY

ANTICHRIST REVEALED TO THE JEWS

(MIDDLE OF WEEK)

ABOMINATION

COSMIC EVENTS OCCUR 6TH SEAL

SHORTENED TRIBULATION

GATHERING OF ELECT

"GREAT MULTITUDE" OF CHRISTIANS THAT "NO MAN COULD NUMBER" RAPTURED AND SEEN IN HEAVEN (REV. 7:9-14)

144,000 JEWS SEALED FROM THE "WRATH OF GOD"

END OF THE 70TH WEEK

BATTLE OF ARMAGEDDON

"WRATH OF GOD" AND THE BEGINNING OF THE "DAY OF THE LORD" UPON ALL UNBELIEVERS

"WRATH OF GOD" STARTS HERE!

7 TRUMPETS

7 VIALS

"DAY OF THE LORD" PERIOD

30 DAYS

Chart 7: Hal Lindsey's Model

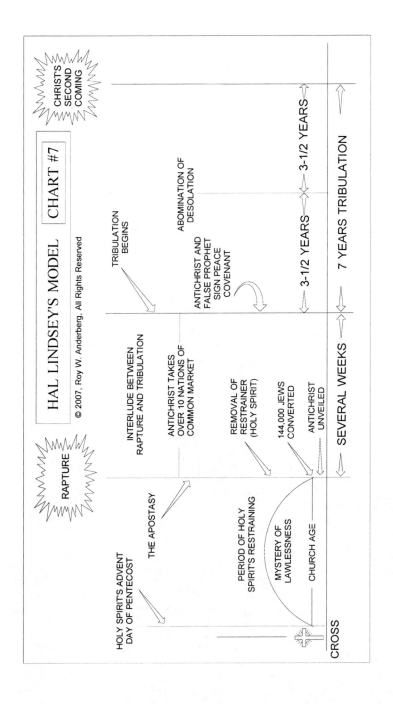

HAL LINDSEY'S MODEL — CHART #7

CHRIST'S SECOND COMING

RAPTURE

TRIBULATION BEGINS

ABOMINATION OF DESOLATION

ANTICHRIST AND FALSE PROPHET SIGN PEACE COVENANT

INTERLUDE BETWEEN RAPTURE AND TRIBULATION

ANTICHRIST TAKES OVER 10 NATIONS OF COMMON MARKET

REMOVAL OF RESTRAINER (HOLY SPIRIT)

144,000 JEWS CONVERTED

ANTICHRIST UNVEILED

THE APOSTASY

HOLY SPIRIT'S ADVENT DAY OF PENTECOST

PERIOD OF HOLY SPIRIT'S RESTRAINING

MYSTERY OF LAWLESSNESS

CHURCH AGE

CROSS

SEVERAL WEEKS

3-1/2 YEARS — 3-1/2 YEARS

7 YEARS TRIBULATION

Chart 8: Post Tribulation Model (Author)

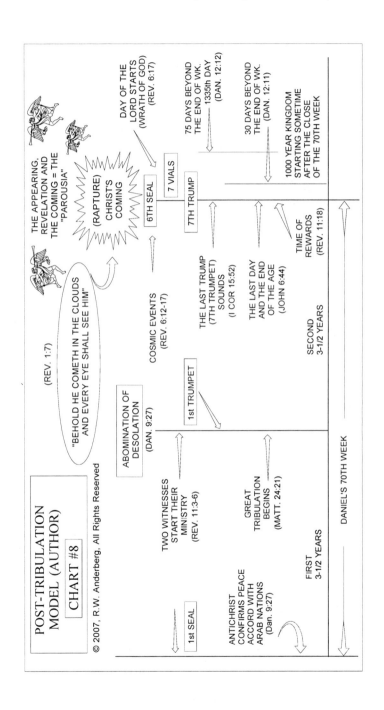

Chart 9: Views of the Day of the Lord

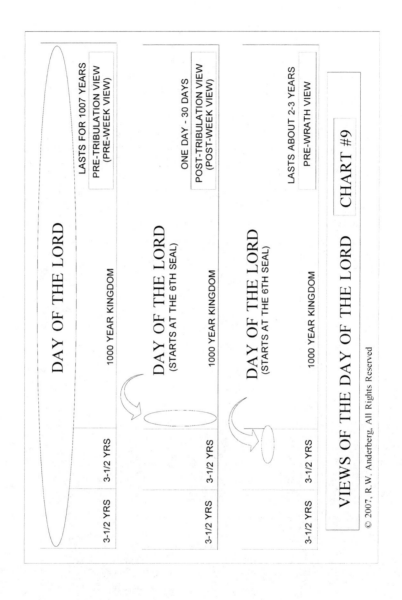

Chart 10: Cosmic Events Take Place at the 6th Seal

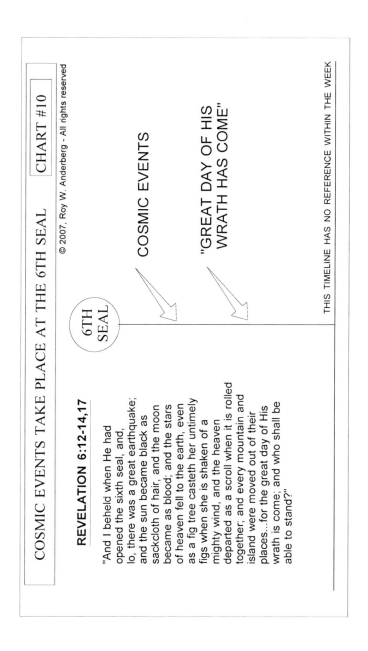

COSMIC EVENTS TAKE PLACE AT THE 6TH SEAL | CHART #10

COSMIC EVENTS

"GREAT DAY OF HIS WRATH HAS COME"

THIS TIMELINE HAS NO REFERENCE WITHIN THE WEEK

6TH SEAL

REVELATION 6:12-14,17

"And I beheld when He had opened the sixth seal, and, lo, there was a great earthquake; and the sun became black as sackcloth of hair, and the moon became as blood; and the stars of heaven fell to the earth, even as a fig tree casteth her untimely figs when she is shaken of a mighty wind, and the heaven departed as a scroll when it is rolled together; and every mountain and island were moved out of their places...for the great day of His wrath is come; and who shall be able to stand?"

Chart 11: Cosmic Events After Great Tribulation

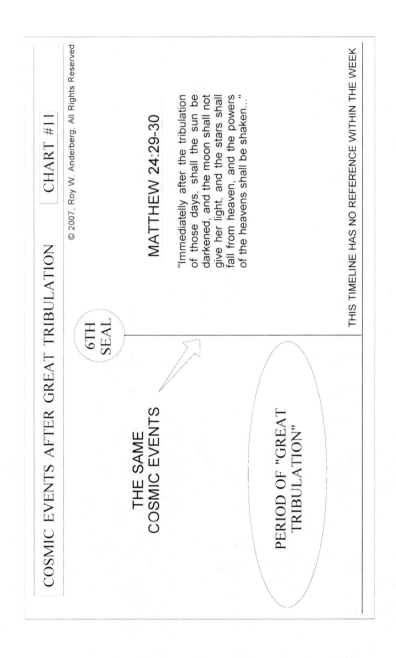

Chart 12: Cosmic Events Before "Day of the Lord"

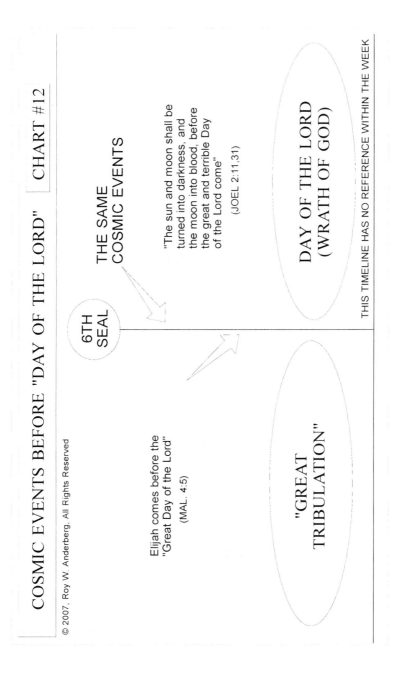

COSMIC EVENTS BEFORE "DAY OF THE LORD" | **CHART #12**

THE SAME COSMIC EVENTS

6TH SEAL

"The sun and moon shall be turned into darkness, and the moon into blood, before the great and terrible Day of the Lord come"

(JOEL 2:11,31)

Elijah comes before the "Great Day of the Lord"

(MAL. 4:5)

"GREAT TRIBULATION"

DAY OF THE LORD (WRATH OF GOD)

THIS TIMELINE HAS NO REFERENCE WITHIN THE WEEK

Chart 13: Christ Comes After the Cosmic Events

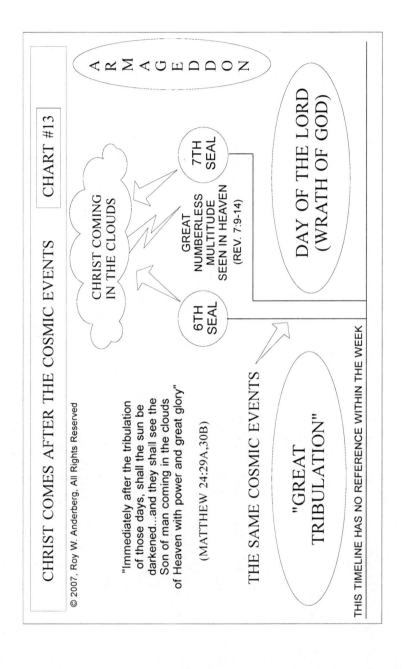

Chart 14: The Same Cosmic Events and Their Relationship Between the Day of the Lord, the 6th Seal, and the Great Tribulation

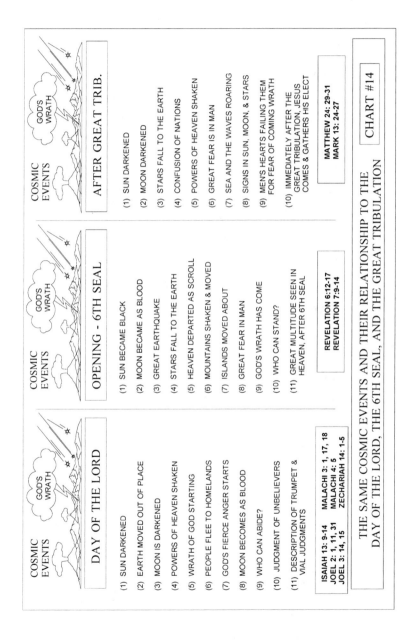

COSMIC EVENTS — GOD'S WRATH

DAY OF THE LORD

(1) SUN DARKENED
(2) EARTH MOVED OUT OF PLACE
(3) MOON IS DARKENED
(4) POWERS OF HEAVEN SHAKEN
(5) WRATH OF GOD STARTING
(6) PEOPLE FLEE TO HOMELANDS
(7) GOD'S FIERCE ANGER STARTS
(8) MOON BECOMES AS BLOOD
(9) WHO CAN ABIDE?
(10) JUDGMENT OF UNBELIEVERS
(11) DESCRIPTION OF TRUMPET & VIAL JUDGMENTS

ISAIAH 13: 9-14 — MALACHI 3: 1, 17, 18
JOEL 2: 1, 11, 31 — MALACHI 4: 5
JOEL 3: 14, 15 — ZECHARIAH 14: 1-5

COSMIC EVENTS — GOD'S WRATH

OPENING - 6TH SEAL

(1) SUN BECAME BLACK
(2) MOON BECAME AS BLOOD
(3) GREAT EARTHQUAKE
(4) STARS FALL TO THE EARTH
(5) HEAVEN DEPARTED AS SCROLL
(6) MOUNTAINS SHAKEN & MOVED
(7) ISLANDS MOVED ABOUT
(8) GREAT FEAR IN MAN
(9) GOD'S WRATH HAS COME
(10) WHO CAN STAND?
(11) GREAT MULTITUDE SEEN IN HEAVEN, AFTER 6TH SEAL

REVELATION 6:12-17
REVELATION 7:9-14

COSMIC EVENTS — GOD'S WRATH

AFTER GREAT TRIB.

(1) SUN DARKENED
(2) MOON DARKENED
(3) STARS FALL TO THE EARTH
(4) CONFUSION OF NATIONS
(5) POWERS OF HEAVEN SHAKEN
(6) GREAT FEAR IS IN MAN
(7) SEA AND THE WAVES ROARING
(8) SIGNS IN SUN, MOON, & STARS
(9) MEN'S HEARTS FAILING THEM FOR FEAR OF COMING WRATH
(10) IMMEDIATELY AFTER THE GREAT TRIBULATION, JESUS COMES & GATHERS HIS ELECT

MATTHEW 24: 29-31
MARK 13: 24-27

THE SAME COSMIC EVENTS AND THEIR RELATIONSHIP TO THE DAY OF THE LORD, THE 6TH SEAL, AND THE GREAT TRIBULATION

CHART #14

and that will not be until the end of the 70th week (Acts 3:19-21). The 70th week of Daniel will surely be included within that time frame. The presence of the Holy Spirit will dwell in the tribulation believers (Rev. 20:4) until their resurrection or rapture, at the end of the week.

4) Another question that arises is; where exactly in scripture does it say, or imply, that Jesus will come down to earth, pick up the Church, go back up into Heaven for 7 years, and then come back down for the rest of His saints at some other time? This conclusion, they say, is taken from John 14:1-3; however, this would seem contrary to a statement that Peter made, *"And he shall send Jesus Christ, which before was preached unto you: whom the heaven must receive until the times of restitution of all things, which God hath spoken by the mouth of all his holy prophets since the world began"* (Acts 3:20-21). Christ will remain in Heaven until its time to restore all things – a very clear statement that He won't come back until the <u>end</u> of the tribulation period. (end of the week, which fulfills Daniel, chapter 9:24). The restoration is at the end of all things, after God's wrath, and certainly <u>not</u> at the beginning of the week, which would seem out of place because Antichrist must have his heyday! (This is a repeat, but the point is important).

5) And lastly, in the pre-tribulation theory, the removal of the Holy Spirit prior at the start of the week would require eight events to take place:

1. the revealing of the *"man of sin"* (Antichrist),

2. the *"apostasy,"*

3. the beginning of the *"day of the Lord,"*

4. the *"time of harvest,"*

5. the *"last day,"*

6. the *"end of the world,"*

7. the *"last trumpet."* (which is when the resurrection occurs) and,

8. the coming of *"Elijah"*

The placement of any of these events at or before the beginning of the 70th week would distort the entire picture of Christ's parousia as well as the timing of the other events.

Dr. Cyrus Scofield (1843-1921, author of the Scofield Study Bible with 1917 notes of II Thessalonians found on "www.studylight.org"), maintained that the Holy Spirit was the only one who could fulfill the role as the restrainer. This conclusion, he said, was through the process of elimination; however that assumption is not necessarily correct – there are other possibilities. It appears to me that there is a lack of evidence or examples in the Bible where the primary role of the Holy Spirit is to fight with fallen angels, contend with Satan and his demons, or act as a restraining power for any person, nation, or thing (the Spirit persuaded Paul not to preach in Asia – Acts 16:1, but that is not the primary role of the Spirit). It is not that the Holy Spirit can't do these things, but rather His role is different than the angels that God created. As part of the triune Godhead, the primary purpose and ministry of the Holy Spirit is:

1) to be a comforter and a teacher to the believer – (Jn. 14:26.)

2) to convict the unsaved of their sin - (Jn. 16:8.)

3) to administer the various gifts to the believer – (I Cor. 12:8.)

4) to spiritually empower all believers and to regenerate them– (Acts 1:4-5; Titus 3:5; Ezek. 36:25)

5) to seal the believer after salvation until the day of redemption – (Eph. 4:30.)

So, to retain the thought that the *"he"* in v.7 is the Holy Spirit, is at best, speculation – especially since we know that there will be a numberless multitude of Christians (Rev. 7:14; 20:4) who will pass through the tribulation and resist paying homage to Antichrist. This numberless multitude represents all nations, and languages and would assuredly need the power and leading of the Holy Spirit. If these people were to lack the sealing and indwelling of the Holy Spirit, they could not be defined as Christians since every believer is indwelled and sealed until the resurrection of the body (Eph. 1:13, 4:30). There are not two plans of salvation and redemption, nor are there two categories of Christians. The first two verses in our text (II Thess. 2:1-2) refutes the idea that the Holy Spirit is removed before the revealing of the man of sin and the apostasy. The natural, unstrained interpretation of the sequence of events in the text under consideration, would be:

- <u>First</u>, the apostasy (the abandonment of a profession of faith in Christ)
- <u>Second</u>, the revealing of the man of sin (Antichrist sitting in the temple as God),
- <u>Third</u>, the gathering of the saints (the rapture),
- <u>Lastly</u>, the day of the Lord's judgment (His wrath upon the wicked unbelievers)

Now let's examine an alternative, for another personage as the restrainer. I will attempt to build a reasonable case for Michael, the chief prince and angelic protector of Israel (Dan.

10:13; 12:1), who is also the archangel in God's mighty angelic army and will be with Christ at His parousia (Jude 9; I Thess. 4:16). In my opinion, Michael could fill the shoes of the "restrainer" quite adequately.

We must not think of the concluding battle between the forces of good and evil which will be fought with nuclear bombs, tanks, aircraft and missiles, but rather in addition, it will be the final encounter of spiritual forces as well (Christ vs. Satan). When Lucifer (Satan) rebelled against God (Isa. 14:6-19; Ezek. 28:11-19), he took with him millions of angels to earth to function as demons. Some of these angels were so wicked that they were placed in chains in everlasting darkness, in Hell, until the day of judgment (Mt. 25:41; Jude: 6). The other angels who were confined, went into the abyss (bottomless pit, deep), only to be released just prior to the coming (parousia) of Christ. The unconfined angels will now function as demons and are at the command of Satan who is the ruler of all demons (Mt. 12:24). Demons are real and powerful; they inflict disease (Lk. 13:16), manipulate and control the mind (II Cor. 4:4), deceive people (Eph. 2:2), and they can even deceive the leaders of nations (Rev. 16:14). In the days when Jesus was upon the earth, there was a tremendous display of demonic activity in opposition to Christ's Messiahship. There is an abundance of scriptural examples as to the power and manifestations of demons indwelling people (Mt. 4:24, 8:28; Lu. 8:27; Rev. 16:14, 18:2, etc.). Demons have no fleshly bodies and are called spirits (Lk. 10:17, 20; Mt. 8:16), but they cannot be in two places at one time, and they apparently have intelligence (they identified Jesus and talked with Him – Lk. 8:28-31).

God has chosen to use His army of holy elect angels (I Tim. 5:21) to accomplish the administration of His divine will amidst people and nations. God's angels have four primarily functions:

1) Defending the holiness of God they minister around the throne of God (Seraphim and Cherubim – the highest order and class of angels with tremendous power and beauty – Isa. 6:1)

2) Restraining evil (one angel can bind Satan – Dan. 10:12-13, 20-21; Rev. 20:1)

3) Administrating God's judgments (II Chron.32:21; Isa. 37:36; Rev. 16:1; Acts 12:23; etc.)

4) Acting as messengers to the saved and unsaved (Gen. 19:15; Dan. 3:28; Mt. 1:20; Acts 8:26)

We see examples of their responsibilities over and over again, both in the Old and New Testaments. We can rightly assume that the *"restrainer"* must be able to work on a spiritual level in order to combat or restrict evil perpetrated by Satan's rebellious angels and his army of demons; and I'm sure we all could agree that human government, although capable of enforcing man-made laws, could not be involved in such powerful spiritual activity, nor could their influence override the will of angels, under the direction of our sovereign God.

After a 70 year period, the Babylonian captivity for the Jews had ended as prophesied by Jeremiah (Dan. 9:2). The Medes and Persians conquered Babylon in about 539 B.C., and king Cyrus of Persia was now in command. The Lord burdened the king to allow the Jews to return to Jerusalem and rebuild the temple. *"Thus saith king Cyrus of Persia, the Lord God of heaven hath given me all the kingdoms of the earth; and He hath charged me to build Him an house at Jerusalem, which is in Judah"* (Ezra 1:2). So adamant was he to do this, that much of the funding for the temple construction eventually came from the Persian treasury. In due course, a decree was made by king Darius, successor of Cyrus, that anyone who interfered with this task was to be put to death by hanging. There was a great deal of opposition to the Jerusalem reconstruction project all of the days of king Cyrus and King Darius, and later on as well, because <u>Satan and his angels</u> were working to prevent the city from being rebuilt and Israel worshipping Jehovah, their God.

In the early years of the reign of king Cyrus (after 70 years of Babylonian captivity), Daniel had several visions and dreams. In one vision, an angel came to Daniel in answer to his prayer, but the angel was three weeks late in coming because of a struggle that he was having with the prince of Persia (an evil angel). God's angel said, *"[12]Fear not, Daniel: for from the first day that thou didst set thine heart to understand, and to chasten thyself before thy God, thy words were heard, and I am come for thy words. [13]But the <u>prince</u> of the kingdom of Persia withstood me one and twenty days: but, lo, Michael, one of the <u>chief princes</u>, came to help me; and I remained there with the kings of Persia"* (Dan. 10:12-13). And after that, the angel announced that he had to go back and fight some more with the evil angel of Persia, and later he was to do battle with the prince (angel) of Greece. *"...[20]Knowest thou wherefore I come unto thee? And now will I return to fight with the <u>prince</u> of Persia: and when I am gone forth, lo, the <u>prince</u> of Greecia shall come. [21]But I will show thee that which is noted in the scripture of truth: and there is none that holdeth with me in these things, but Michael your <u>prince</u>"* (Dan. 10:20-21). We can see from scripture that "princes" (angels) fight against other angels. Re-examining our challenging text of who the restrainer is, we conclude that Michael, the archangel, could easily restrain certain angels and limit events that would harm Israel, until the "appointed" time that God comes to redeem the earth and rule it with a rod of iron.

I also have another thought on the subject of angels fighting and restraining. If there is an angel assigned to Persia, Greece, and Israel, is it not conceivable that there is one of God's "princes" also (or perhaps many), assigned to protect America and England and also to have present, Satan's evil angels attempting to counter God's will? If we are willing to be open minded, and expand our thinking outside the standard theological box, it may be viewed as possible that the "princes" of America and England will be the restraining power along with Michael, and will step aside when told to do so by God, ushering in the revealing of the man of sin (Antichrist) to persecute Israel and all Christians everywhere.

To sum up my thoughts on the identity of the restrainer, I feel that the archangel, Michael and his army of angels, would be a logical and competing choice since that is the natural role assigned to angels; it would also fulfill the neuter and the masculine requirement of our text. I am aware that if you hold to the pre-trib position, you would like to see the restrainer as the Holy Spirit, but scripture should support our conclusions as much as possible. Again, if Paul meant the restrainer to be the Holy Spirit, why didn't he simply say the word "Spirit" as he did 6 verses later? Many students of prophecy have trouble removing the Church at the beginning of the week, as well as the Holy Spirit, and still have millions of people somehow getting saved at lightning speed, all without the indwelling and sealing of the Spirit. And if you believe that Pentecost will somehow be reversed, then we need scripture in the New Testament to support such a radical thought.

The Blessed Hope and the Rapture

(the physical appearing of Christ for His saints)

Again, we repeat what the writer of Titus said, *"Looking for that <u>blessed hope, and the glorious appearing</u> of the great God and our Saviour Jesus Christ..."* (2:13). I look forward to the blessed resurrection and His physical appearing. Some would have us to think that by not holding to the idea of imminence, and by passing through the tribulation, it would somehow render meaningless the hope of looking for Christ's appearing; nothing could be further from the truth, and in fact, a case could be made for that "blessed hope" becoming even more blessed.

Would you tell an expectant mother that the vision and dream of holding her newborn child is really no hope at all because of the pain she is going to go through just before delivery? That would be foolish! She is not looking forward to the pain, but what the completion of the pain will bring forth. Her concentration is on the "<u>expectancy</u>" of the birth. She has prepared the baby's room for this new arrival; she has told all her friends; she is excited. And so it is with me personally, I am not looking forward to tribulation, but the glorious appearing of my Saviour (and at my age, also a new body). We in America, and in the West, have a deformed mindset when it comes to serving Christ. We sit in our mega-churches on padded pews, heated and air conditioned buildings with stained glass windows, carpeted floors, nice new hymnbooks, full "worship teams playing copyrighted tunes," paid staff, and we are fully dressed and ready for the blessing of the "fast food" 30 minute

Western style sermonette (it needs to be 30 minutes or less because we need to get home and tend to the roast we have cooking in the oven). What a distortion and aberration of the true persecuted Church in the real world of Christianity. Millions of Christians in other nations are suffering torture, hardship, and death, because of the antichrist's that surround them. Christians are arrested and beaten on a regular basis and still sing the old hymns of glory. Their vision of the *"blessed hope and glorious appearing"* of Christ, is so much more real than ours. They are not looking for the tribulation; they are already in it! They are looking beyond their pain and for Christ to come in the clouds; in the brilliant skies with all of the saints and holy angels; that's the way the persecuted Church has always been. They knew that they would be passing through tribulation before their Saviour returned. They were comforted when Paul told them, *"⁷And to you who are troubled rest with us, when the Lord Jesus shall be revealed from heaven with his mighty angels, ⁸In flaming fire <u>taking vengeance on them that know not God</u>, and that obey not the gospel of our Lord Jesus Christ: ⁹Who shall be punished with everlasting destruction from the presence of the Lord, and from the glory of his power; ¹⁰<u>When he shall come to be glorified in his saints</u>, and to be admired in all them that believe (because our testimony among you was believed) <u>in that day</u>"* (II Thess. 1:7-10). It is very apparent here, that the disciples comfort and release from their immediate trials and troubles will come only in a post-tribulational setting, that is, when Christ comes with His angels to punish the world, *"<u>in that day</u>."* The rest and the revelation of Christ cannot be separated. So, to suggest that the blessed hope of Christ's appearing is anything other than a "blessed hope" to the Christians, is a very unrealistic thought.

John 14:1-3

This is a text that is frequently used to support a pre-tribulation "silent, secret, any moment" rapture. John says, *"¹Let not your heart be troubled: ye believe in God, believe also in me. In my Father's house are many mansions: if it were not so, I would have told you. ²I go to prepare a place for you. ³And if I go and prepare a place for you, I will come again, and receive you unto myself; that where I am, there ye may be also."*

Tim Lehaye in his book, *"No Fear of the Storm,"* says that these verses teach an "any moment" coming, without signs. He says, *"The promise that our Lord could appear any moment to take His Church up to His Father's house was delivered by the Lord Himself (see John 14:1-3)."* I'm sorry, but I seem to be missing something here! Using the normal and correct hermeneutical interpretation of this passage, I would ask two questions:

1) Where does it say or imply that the His coming will happen at "any moment?"

2) Where does it say that He will take the "Church" to Heaven?

This passage has no connection to the timing of the rapture whatsoever. The emphasis in this passage is on the fact that wherever Jesus is, we will be there with Him. Jesus is simply making a statement that He is preparing special residences for us, while also stating that there are already many mansions or rooms up there. There is nothing in the text to suggest that we will be going to Heaven in the rapture. We must remember the main reason for glorified bodies is so that the ones that we will be ruling and reigning over, can see us; you can't see a spirit. We will be like the angels and will be able to manifest ourselves in bodies. Tim Lehaye's interpretation, and others holding his view, believe that this is a proof text of a pre-week rapture – that is pure supposition! This text certainly doesn't teach the "any moment rapture theory," nor is it clear that the Church even goes to Heaven, but only that we will be with Jesus at His coming. The question should be, "where will Christ be when He returns and where does the Bible say that He will He reside after that?" These "mansions" may very well be in the *"New Jerusalem"* which will be coming down from God out of Heaven (Rev. 21:2) that we will be occupying in our resurrected bodies. We do not have to go up there to occupy them. Besides, would it make sense to go up to Heaven for 7 years, occupy our mansions, and then vacate them for another thousand to reign on earth, especially when we know that the judgment and rewards are at the end of the 70th week and here on earth (II Tim. 4:1, 8, etc.)?

When the parousia of Christ occurs, Jesus will be with us forever in the New Jerusalem; that's where the mansions are and that's where He is. When Christ comes down from Heaven, and the last of His judgments are completed, He will be staying on earth, not in Heaven. The New Jerusalem City is, *"prepared as a bride adorned for her husband."* Jesus, and all of the redeemed will be reigning together on earth during the millennial period, and there will be no need to return to God's abode in the 3rd Heaven (II Cor. 12:2). We find that Revelation, chapter 21, does not chronically follow previous chapters. In verse 9 of chapter 21, John said, *"And there came unto me one of the seven angels which had the seven vials full of the seven last plagues, and talked with me, saying, come hither, I will show thee the bride, the Lamb's wife."* Notice that the seven vials are full! But in chapter 16, they were already dispensed. After that, the angel showed John a picture of the New Jerusalem which was soon to come down from Heaven; notice also, that the tears will be wiped away at the time the New Jerusalem City arrives, and some think that chapter 21 is at the end of the 1000 years, but why would God be wiping away the tears if we have already been reigning with Him for the 1000 years? This is a picture of what the saved saints will experience during the 1000 years in the kingdom. We will have glorified bodies, immortal and incorruptible and residing in our new mansions.

Is Post-Trib Really a "Yo-Yo" Rapture?

No! When Jesus comes with the <u>souls</u> of the saints, to be re-united with their bodies (II Thess. 3:13; Mal. 3:17-18; Zech. 14:5; Jude 14), He will raise up all of the saints from their graves at once (Job 14:13; Isa. 26:19-21; Ps. 17: Dan.12:1, etc.). But we don't really know how long He will be in the air before coming down to the Mount of Olives (where He ascended - Acts 1:9-11), or how far from Heaven He will be when He raptures us. If the vials are dispensed in one literal day, we would be taken up immediately before the first one, and be with Him from then on wherever He is. Who is to say how long it will take Jesus to descend to the earth so that every eye can see Him? (Rev. 1:7); maybe He stays in the air for a period of time for a dramatic effect, who really knows? Or maybe, now that the rapture has occurred and we are like the angels, we will be in the air until all of the battles are completed. The pre-trib advocates call a post-tribulation parousia, the "yo-yo" effect, that is, they think that the saints are meeting Christ in the air, going back to Heaven and then coming right back down. But let's think about this for a moment. If this is the way it really is, and I don't believe it, who are we to mock God by questioning His sovereignty and making a joke about His method of rapture? God can do what

He wants, when He wants, and How He wants. Maybe that is why Paul calls the resurrection and change of the body a "mystery" (I Cor. 15:51). But in reality, we are not actually going up to Heaven and coming back down, because we will be coming down from Heaven to begin with as souls. All of the millions and millions of deceased souls of the Old and New Testament will just continue on down to rule and reign with Him, possessing our new bodies while still in the air. That certainly can happen in a moment of time just like the resurrection. What reason would we have to return to Heaven if Jesus is not there? The rewarding of believers takes place here on earth and are not given out during the tribulation as most pre-tribbers teach (II Tim. 4:1, 8; Mt. 16:27, Rev. 11:18, etc.). If Christ chooses to unite our souls with our decayed bodies to make a glorified body on the way down, that's His prerogative. Can you honestly call this a "yo-yo" effect? This "yo-yo" argument is ridiculous to use anyway if you are trying to defend against the historical Church view of a single parousia at the end of the week.

In Acts, chapter 3, and verses 19-21, Peter clearly said that Christ will remain up in Heaven until the restitution of all things. It appears that Christ will not go back up to Heaven! Does one think that meeting Him in the air, and then continuing on down to earth, is any more unreasonable than the pre-trib rapture theory. In the pre-trib rapture scenario, Christ comes down, raptures the saints, does an immediate "U-turn" and returns to Heaven for 7 years. Then they abandon their mansions after a brief 7 years, and come right back down for another 1000 years to be judged and rewarded; that seems to be a more awkward position to defend than the traditional post-trib parousia which Jesus taught; so, I certainly would not be dogmatic regarding any of the events that transpire after

Christ's parousia; they simply have not been revealed to us yet. But we do know for sure, that the rewards are given out:

- at the return of Jesus (Rev. 22:12; Isa. 40:10; Mt. 16:27)
- after the resurrection (Lk. 14:14)
- after the 7th trumpet (Rev. 11:18)
- at His appearing (II Tim. 4:1, 8; I Pet. 5:4)
- at the kingdom setup (II Tim. 4:1, 8; Lu. 14:14)

So however long that takes (which may be completed in seconds like our sudden immortal body change), that's the way it is. Perhaps it will be like a dream. Have you ever had a dream that seemed to be as long as a full length movie? Researchers tell us that dreams last only in seconds, or at the most minutes, but yet it seems in our minds to be hours or days; but in God's realm, there is no time in the way that humans think. In our new glorified bodies, we will experience things in quite a different way. Perhaps God will give out the rewards all at once, and place them in our minds – bingo! – it's done! And we must not rule out the possibility that the individual judgment and accounting of believers may take place immediately after we die and go to Heaven as souls. Does anyone think that we still have a recognition of sin, guilt, or sorrow resulting from our past behavior on earth after we are with Christ in Heaven? If a dear saint died 500 years ago, does that mean that he is in Heaven still with his sins on his mind and in misery? I don't think so. Standing before a holy and righteous God to give a personal accounting as individuals will be humbling enough. Think about the shame we will feel if not having served well. I don't think it is God's purpose to "flash" our past in front of all the other saints in Heaven to compare who was the worst. Who really dogmatically knows about these things of God? Our human reasoning must be discarded when it comes to matters of the unknown, thus, we must rest with contentment on the scriptures which are clear – and there are lots of them.

Will Any Unsaved Gentiles Enter the 1000 Year Kingdom?

There is little doubt in my mind that there will be many unsaved men, women, and children who will enter the kingdom period who are "leftovers" from the global judgments, perhaps having never heard of Jesus Christ. However, the pre-trib adherents believe and teach with great conviction, that no unbelievers will enter the 1000 year kingdom of Christ – that belief becomes <u>necessary</u> if you believe in two parousia's (comings) of Christ. In addition, most teach that the Christians who are in the tribulation period will <u>not</u> have glorified bodies, and will enter the kingdom as mortals bearing children that produce the wicked offspring who come against Jerusalem at the end of the millennial kingdom. John MacAuthur states, *"Isn't everybody a believer? No, <u>the only people who enter the Kingdom will be believers.</u> They will be the sheep in the judgments of Matthew 24 and 25, in the Olivet Discourse, the sheep who enter into the Kingdom. Only believers will enter the Kingdom, because when Christ returns, He'll destroy all the ungodly. <u>Only believers will enter, but many of them, of course, will still be in their physical bodies; and all of them who enter the Kingdom immediately, on earth, will be physically alive. And so, they will reproduce and have children."</u>(tape-GC-66-76 – www.biblebb.com/files/MAC/66-76.htm).*

It is MacAuthur's teaching (and most pre-tribulationalists), that millions of people during the *"7 year tribulation period"* (a non-biblical term that is used instead of the "70th week") become saved after the rapture. No where in the Bible is there mentioned a 7 year tribulation period. And certainly there is no place recorded in scripture where it indicates that Gentiles become saved during that period; let alone enter the kingdom with non-glorified physical bodies bearing evil children. By holding to a pre-week coming, it is necessary that Christians produce millions of offspring who will rebel against God at the end of the 1000 years. In my opinion, that theory is the most absurd theology that I have ever heard of concerning an end time scenario. Because pre-trib people do not allow for leftover tribulation <u>unbelievers</u> to enter the kingdom, they have no other option of reasoning as to where this great number of rebellious sinners will come from. It is my argument, that the great multitude of seditious sinners will come from the offspring of <u>unbelievers</u> in the nations that God allows to enter the kingdom. These unbelievers will be ruled over with a rod of iron by Christ and His saints right from the <u>beginning</u> of the 1000 years. If the saints are ruling and reigning with Christ with a *"rod of iron"* during <u>all</u> of the 1000 years, like it says in Revelation 20, then where do you think all of these people and nations come from? John said, *"And out of his mouth goeth a sharp sword, that with it he should <u>smite the nations: and he shall rule them with a rod of iron</u>: and he treadeth the winepress of the fierceness and wrath of Almighty God."* (Rev. 19:15). In this advent text, we see that God *"smites"* the nations and then He says that He will *"rule them with a rod of iron."* A reasonable question would be: How could Christ rule the nations if He just destroyed them? It should seem obvious that He didn't kill every living soul on earth. Again, in context, the word smite demands to mean: to inflict damage by way of a sword, to afflict, or to inflict with diseases or pestilence, etc. The Greek word used here is, "Patasso" (pat-as'-so) and besides death, it can have the lesser meaning of affliction rather than complete destruction resulting in death. All of the nations are <u>not</u> destroyed at His parousia; punished – yes! But annihilated – No!

Scripture tells us that God allows many of these leftover unbelievers to go back to their countries of origin to tell the folks back home about the tremendous power and glory of Jesus Christ, and how the Jews suddenly become rescued and protected by their Messiah and King, Jesus Christ. Many of these may still remain sinners just as there were in the day when Christ performed miracles and they attributed His works to Satan. But it is also possible that they will acknowledge Christ as King of the earth and will go into Jerusalem and worship Him, but their offspring will side with Satan in the final end.

The problem with believing that Christians will produce the wicked people who rebel against God, is that the basic premise is wrong. Jesus absolutely declares His parousia (coming) to be at the end of the week, and because it is only a <u>single</u> one time event, no Gentile Christians will be entering the kingdom in mortal bodies, which is just the opposite of what pre-trib proponents believe. All believers have the same intrinsic promises of God – namely, that <u>all believers</u> will be raised or raptured and become immortal; therefore <u>no</u> Gentile believers can enter the kingdom in mortal bodies. The idea of mortal Christians entering the kingdom in mortal bodies is in direct conflict with Paul's resurrection statement about all Christians, and certainly this would apply to the tribulation saints who were martyred for the Gospel of Christ. Paul said concerning the believers body, *"[44]It is sown a natural body; it is raised a spiritual body...[51]Behold I show you a mystery; we shall not all sleep, but we shall all be changed, [52]in a moment, in the twinkling of any eye, at the last trump, for the trumpet shall sound, and the dead shall be raised incorruptible, and we shall be changed."* (I Cor. 15:44, 51-52). Paul made no distinction between another group of "lesser privileged," second rate believers. The saints who live or die during the tribulation will most certainly have glorified bodies and are included in the first resurrection, which occurs at the end of the great tribulation (Rev. 20:4-6). There is not even vague scriptural support to show that some believers receive glorified bodies and other "types" of believing Gentiles do not. To not include the Gentile tribulation saints in the first resurrection and to reduce their status to mere reigning mortals is an insult to the integrity of the Holy Writ.

There are various passages of scripture that suggest that millions of unsaved (and perhaps one third of the world) will go into the kingdom. One passage is absolutely irrefutable; I will start with that one. In the book of Zechariah, chapter 14, we have Jesus announcing the coming of the *"day of the Lord"* at the end of the week. He gathers all the nations against Jerusalem for a battle; they take the city captive, and on the imminent *"day of the Lord,"* Jesus fights for His chosen ones by splitting the mountains at Jerusalem just before His return, thus creating a large valley for the remnant to escape (the valley of Azal). Next, he announces His coming to the Mount of Olives with all of His saints, and the battle of Armageddon begins (Zec. 14:4-12). After the battle, the prophet announces that God will punish the nations that fought against Jerusalem: He says, *"And this shall be the plague wherewith the LORD will smite all the people that have fought against Jerusalem; Their flesh shall consume away while they stand upon their feet, and their eyes shall consume away in their holes, and their tongue shall consume away in their mouth"* (v.12); but also God allows many unsaved to enter the kingdom, as previously mentioned.

An example of the way "all" is used to mean "most" would be: *"America and its allies destroyed all of Hitler's army."* Now that doesn't mean that every German soldier and officer was killed. There were many, many that were taken prisoner, but the main army was effectively defeated and destroyed. They were rendered totally helpless.

That thought brings us to our next text that confirms that many unbelievers will enter the kingdom. Zechariah states, *"¹⁶And it shall come to pass, that <u>every one that is left of all the nations which came against Jerusalem</u> shall even go up from year to year to worship the King, the LORD of hosts, and to keep the feast of tabernacles. ¹⁷And it shall be, that whoso will not come up of all the families of the earth unto Jerusalem to worship the King, the LORD of hosts, even upon them shall be no rain. ¹⁸And if the family of Egypt go not up, and come not, that have no rain; there shall be the plague, wherewith the LORD will smite the heathen that come not up to keep the feast of tabernacles. ¹⁹<u>This shall be the punishment of Egypt, and the punishment of all nations that come not up to keep the feast of tabernacles</u>"* (Zec. 16-19). Not only are there unsaved individuals, but many nations are represented in the ones that go into the kingdom; our text said, *"...every one that is left of all the nations..."* and then again in verse 17, *"all the families of the earth..."* The text cannot be any clearer, these are large numbers of unsaved nations and people present when the earth is restored. Also, verse 16 indicates a punitive action if these leftover people do not worship Christ. If only Christians were entering, it would not be necessary to threaten them. God receives His righteous glory and honor, by allowing the non-believers to witness the rescue and salvation of Israel and all righteous glorified believers who will rule over them with a *"rod of iron."* We rule over the unsaved for 1000 years, and not a year less; again, who would we be reigning over with a *"rod of iron"* if it wasn't the unsaved who God allowed to enter the kingdom? We start our reign on the very first day of the 1000 year kingdom, whenever that day begins.

We find other evidence in scripture, that suggests God allows these unsaved people to go into the kingdom, bringing us to the next example. In chapters 4 and 5, of the book of Micah, (a contemporary prophet with Isaiah), we have an explicit setting of the millennial kingdom period. We read about Christ setting up His house in Jerusalem, with nations coming to learn about His ways (thus, insinuating that they do not know about Him – Mic. 4:1-3). Then we see Christ judging and rebuking nations in distant lands and many people worshipping their own gods. Micah declares,

"³And He shall judge among many people, and rebuke strong nations afar off; and they shall beat their swords into plowshares, and their spears into pruning hooks: nation shall not lift up a sword against nation, neither shall they learn war any more. ⁴But they shall sit every man under his vine and under his fig tree; and none shall make them afraid: (because there will be no more war, which will take effect immediately after Armageddon) *for the mouth of the LORD of hosts hath spoken it. ⁵For all people will walk every one in the name of his god, and we will walk in the name of the LORD our God for ever and ever. ⁶In that day, saith the LORD, will I assemble her that halteth, and I will gather her that is driven out, and her that I have afflicted..."* (Mic. 4:3-6). Christ is assembling Abraham's seed of promise, and is allowing others to worship their own foolish gods. It is the offspring of these people who still worship other gods, and who eventually rebel against King Je-

sus and want nothing to do with being the subjects of His kingdom. God does not "shove His love down their throats" and force them to believe, but rather desires that they come to worship Him and learn of His ways. Peter reaffirmed the amazing grace of Christ by declaring, *"The Lord is not slack concerning his promise, as some men count slackness; but is longsuffering to us-ward, <u>not willing that any should perish</u>, but that all should come to repentance"* (II Pet. 3:9). Christ then confirms that this is in the beginning of the kingdom by saying, *"⁷And I will make her that halted a remnant, and her that was cast far off a strong nation: <u>and the LORD shall reign over them in mount Zion from henceforth</u>, even for ever"* (v.7). The phrase, *"from henceforth"* in verse 7, would seem to indicate the beginning of His physical kingdom, and the end of man's rule over the earth.

In the book of Ezekiel, in another post week setting, we have further evidence that the unsaved will enter the kingdom to witness the glory of God. The prophet said, *"³⁵And they shall say, this land that was desolate is become like the garden of Eden; and the waste and desolate and ruined cities are become fenced, and are inhabited. ³⁶<u>Then the heathen that are left round about you shall know that I the LORD build the ruined places, and plant that that was desolate</u>...²⁸And the <u>heathen</u> shall know that I the Lord do sanctify Israel, when my sanctuary shall be in the midst of them for evermore"* (Ezek. 36:35-36; 37:28). These unbelievers remember the way it was before the ravishes of Satan and Antichrist and then saw manifestations of God's judgments (Rev. 15:4); but now they see that Israel is rescued, blessed, and eternally protected by Christ. They weren't getting their information from history books, or some verbal hand-me-down story – they were present and were eye witnesses to the desolation of Israel and then their deliverance. This passage, as well as others, remind us that most of the action will be in the Middle East.

In Isaiah, there are several texts that imply that Egypt *"in that day"* shall be saved and come to know the Lord's ways. The entire 19th chapter deals with the *"burden"* of Egypt, or the judgment and salvation of that nation. Here we have reasonable evidence that Egypt was not an offspring of Christians, but rather one of the leftover nations allowed to remain in Christ's earthly kingdom. First, we see the judgment of Egypt described by Isaiah, *"14The LORD hath mingled a perverse spirit in the midst thereof: and they have caused Egypt to err in every work thereof, as a drunken man staggereth in his vomit... 16In that day shall Egypt be like unto women: and it shall be afraid and fear because of the shaking of the hand of the LORD of hosts, which he shaketh over it. 17And the land of Judah shall be a terror unto Egypt..."* Obviously, the only time that the land of Judah could be a *"terror"* to Egypt would be after the tribulation period when Christ comes back. God judges Egypt (who has a peace treaty with Israel as of the writing of this book), and then after the tribulation is over, we see the healing of that nation. We read a few verses later, *"24In that day shall Israel be the third with Egypt and with Assyria* (modern day Iraq), *even a blessing in the midst of the land: 25Whom the LORD of hosts shall bless, saying, Blessed be Egypt my people, and Assyria the work of my hands, and Israel mine inheritance."* Here we see Egypt and Assyria (Iraq), being blessed after their punishment, and favored in the eyes of God.

In Isaiah chapter 33, an acknowledged millennial passage by most students of the Word, the prophet says, *"9Hear, ye that are far off, what I have done; and, ye that are near, acknowl-*

edge My might." Here is an inference that there are unsaved people in far off nations who have heard of God's judgment and His tremendous power but also the one who rescued Israel. Then Isaiah tells the ones that were very close to the action to *"acknowledge my might;"* so all of these people who were not saved, would become witnesses back in their own homelands (Micah 4:1-5). God would not have to tell believers to *"acknowledge My might,"* for they already stand in awe of His salvation and deliverance. Also, we see that the nations will serve Israel shortly after the return of Christ. Isaiah declares, *"*[10]*And the sons of strangers shall build up thy walls, and their kings shall minister unto thee: for in my wrath I smote thee, but in my favor have I had mercy on thee. *[11]*Therefore thy gates shall be open continually; they shall not be shut day nor night; that men may bring unto thee the forces* (strength, power) *of the Gentiles, and that their kings may be brought. *[12]*For the nation and kingdom that will not serve thee shall perish; yea, those nations shall be utterly wasted...*[14]*The sons also of them that afflicted thee shall come bending unto thee; and all they that despised thee shall bow themselves down at the soles of thy feet; and they shall call thee, The city of the LORD, The Zion of the Holy One of Israel"* (Isa. 60:10-13, 14). It seems apparent that the nations and people that *"afflicted"* Israel, could not have been the offspring of Christians because out text is referring to a past action, *"them that afflicted thee"* (e.g.- during the tribulation). It would also seem unlikely, that the phrases *"the sons of strangers"* and *"their kings"* (in v.10), would refer to Christians or their offspring at the beginning of the kingdom. Perhaps the phrase, *"*[4]*sons of strangers"* would indicate that most of their fathers died in judgment and battle and their sons will learn the ways of the Lord and abandon the ways of war. Isaiah 2:4-5 may reflect that thought, *"⁴And he shall judge among the nations, and shall rebuke many people: and they shall beat their swords into plowshares, and their spears into pruning hooks: nation shall not lift up sword against nation, neither shall they learn war any more. ⁵O house of Jacob, come ye, and let us walk in the light of the LORD."*

In chapter 66 of Isaiah, we find a great number of the unsaved entering the kingdom after the rapture and resurrection (remember, Christ said that they will see Him coming in the clouds immediately <u>after</u> the tribulation and that all of the people of the earth will lament at His coming – Rev. 1:7-8). Isaiah announces, *"¹⁵For, behold, the LORD will come with fire, and with his chariots like a whirlwind, to render his anger with fury, and his rebuke with flames of fire. ¹⁶For by fire and by his sword will the LORD plead with all flesh: and the slain of the LORD shall be many...¹⁸For I know their works and their thoughts: it shall come, that I will gather all nations and tongues; and they shall come up and see my glory. ¹⁹And I will set a sign among them, and <u>I will send those that escape of them unto the nations</u>, to Tarshish, Pul, and Lud, that draw the bow, to Tubal, and Javan, to the isles afar off, that have not heard my fame, neither have seen my glory; and <u>they shall declare my glory among the Gentiles</u>."* Here we see again, that God allows millions of unbelievers who witnessed the judgments of destruction and the re-establishment of Israel, to go back into their lands to declare the glory of God. Christ says, while in total control, *"I will send those that escape..."* All of these nations will be serving the chosen people of Israel or they will perish. We must also remember that all the ones that took the mark, number, or name of Antichrist, will be destined for hell <u>after</u> they die, and their offspring will be amongst those that side with Satan in the end of the kingdom. When the 1st vial (bowl) was dispensed by the angel, the ones that took the mark were not killed, but rather suffered physical pain with putrid sores. Our text says, *"And the first went, and poured out his vial upon the earth; and there fell a noisome* (offensively noxious smell or stinking) *and grievous* (painful) *sore upon the men which had the mark of the beast, and upon them which worshipped his image"* (Rev. 16:2). These people and other un-believers, with their offspring, will be the ones that Christ and all believers, will rule over; notice that He doesn't kill all of them, but will use them for His glory. John proclaims, *"And out of his mouth goeth a sharp sword, that with it he should smite* (break, punish, chasten) *the nations: and he shall rule them with a rod of iron: and he treadeth the winepress of the fierce-ness and wrath of Almighty God."* (Rev. 19:15). This event will be most likely be accomplished shortly after the final plagues are administered and the 1335th day arrives (Dan. 12:12). There will also be unsaved pregnant women in various nations that will give birth to the unsaved, and they to will grow up in the kingdom – some of their offspring will also rebel against the reign of Christ, but many will become sheep in the kingdom.

We know also from Romans, chapter 11, that the remnant of Israel will be saved after Jesus returns, so there will be no un-saved Jews during the kingdom either, but they will have mor-tal bodies because they don't get raptured or resurrected unless they were saved by the blood of Christ prior to the rapture and resurrection. Paul said, *"25For I would not, brethren, that ye should be ignorant of this mystery, lest ye should be wise in your own conceits; that blindness in part is happened to Israel, until the fulness of the Gentiles be come in. 26And so all Israel shall be saved: as it is written, There shall come out of Zion the*

Deliverer, and shall turn away ungodliness from Jacob: <u>*²⁷For this is my covenant unto them, when I shall take away their sins.*</u>" The prophet Ezekiel also tells us, that in addition to Israel being saved and loved by God, all of their offspring born during the millennial kingdom will be righteous as well; he says, *"²³Neither will they defile themselves anymore with their idols and their detestable things, nor with their transgressions: but I will save them out of all their dwelling places, wherein they have sinned, and will cleanse them: so shall they be my people, and I will be their God…²⁶even they and their children and their children's children for ever…"* (Ezek. 37:23, 26). We know from scripture that no unbelievers will come from the seed of the Jews after the tribulation, for God said, *"As for me, this is my covenant with them* (Israel), *saith the LORD; My spirit that is upon thee, and my words which I have put in thy mouth, shall not depart out of thy mouth, nor out of the mouth of thy seed,* <u>*nor out of the mouth of thy seed's seed*</u>*, saith the LORD, from henceforth and* <u>*for ever*</u>" (Isa. 59.21). Further proof that the offspring of the Jews are saved during the kingdom period, is found also in Isaiah: *"³For I will pour water upon him that is thirsty, and floods upon the dry ground: I will pour my spirit upon thy seed, and* <u>*my blessing upon thine offspring*</u>*: ⁴And they shall spring up as among the grass, as willows by the water courses.* (Isa. 44:3-4). And again, in another millennial passage of scripture, *"²³They shall not labour in vain, nor bring forth for trouble; for they are* <u>*the seed of the blessed of the LORD, and their offspring with them.*</u> *²⁴And it shall come to pass, that before they call, I will answer; and while they are yet speaking, I will hear. ²⁵The wolf and the lamb shall feed together, and the lion shall eat straw like the bullock: and dust shall be the serpent's meat. They shall not hurt nor destroy in all my holy* *mountain, saith the LORD"* (Isa. 65:23-25). He then says, *"And all thy children shall be taught of the Lord; and great shall be the peace of thy children. In righteousness shalt thou be established..."* (Isa. 54:13). And finally, to remove any doubt about the seed of Israel being righteous during millennial kingdom and beyond, Isaiah declares, *"In the LORD shall all the seed of Israel be justified, and shall glory"* (Isa. 45:25). All of the *"seed"* is their future seed as well.

All of this is the fulfillment of God's promise in the book of Hebrews, where God says, *"[10]For this is the covenant that I will make with the house of Israel after those days, saith the Lord; I will put my laws into their mind, and write them in their hearts: and I will be to them a God, and they shall be to me a people: [11]And they shall not teach every man his neighbor, and every man his brother, saying, Know the Lord: for all shall know me, from the least to the greatest. [12]For I will be merciful to their unrighteousness, and their sins and their iniquities will I remember no more"* (Heb. 8:10-12).

So, to support the idea that the offspring of <u>Christians</u> or <u>Jews</u> are the wicked ones coming up against Jerusalem at the end of the kingdom period, seems to significantly resist the teachings of Paul, the Apostles and the prophets; especially in light of the scriptures just placed before us. It is my viewpoint that the ones gathering against Israel at the end of the kingdom period, will be the offspring of millions of Gentiles who were left over from God's wrath (the sinners during the millennium - Isa. 65:20). Many of these survivors who went back into their own country will continue to worship other gods (Micah. 4:1-5) and will go to hell when they die. All of the wicked will have been judged by death, or by the vials and Armageddon, but their actual sentence will not be carried out until the great white throne judgment where their works will send them to the lake of fire (Rev. 20:11-15). Remember, God will use many nations and people to serve Israel. The book of Isaiah has many passages, some of them previously mentioned. The nation of Israel is the apple of God's eye, and are an elect people; therefore God will completely rescue them from all of the enemies – that's what the kingdom is all about, to fulfill prophecy.

The Sheep and the Goat Judgment (Matthew 25:31-46)

This is a very difficult passage for all pre-millennialists, including pre-tribulationists and post-tribulationists, because God favors certain people and allows them to enter the kingdom, while others are sent to Hell. This separation is seemingly based upon their works; specific acts or deeds that people have done or have not done. The scriptures clearly teach that salvation on this side of the tribulation is by God's grace through faith; there is no other way. We read in the book of Romans, *"For by grace are ye saved through faith; and that not of yourselves: it is the gift of God: not of works, lest any man should boast"* (Eph. 2:8-9). And again in Ephesians, *"Not by works of righteousness which we have done, but according to his mercy he saved us, by the washing of regeneration, and renewing of the Holy Ghost..."* (Titus 3:5). Paul reiterates that thought by emphasizing that it is the grace of God through the shed blood of His Son that saves us, *"...In whom we have redemption through his blood, even the forgiveness of sins..."* (Col. 1:14). With that in mind, let us look at the complete text which is found in Matthew 25:31-46, and make a few comments and observations:

"³¹When the Son of man shall come in his glory, and all the holy angels with him, then shall he sit upon the throne of his glory: ³²And before him shall be gathered all nations: and he

shall separate them one from another, as a shepherd divideth his sheep from the goats: ³³*And he shall set the sheep on his right hand, but the goats on the left.* ³⁴*Then shall the King say unto them on his right hand, Come, ye blessed of my Father, inherit the kingdom prepared for you from the foundation of the world:* ³⁵*For I was an hungered, and ye gave me meat: I was thirsty, and ye gave me drink: I was a stranger, and ye took me in:*³⁶*Naked, and ye clothed me: I was sick, and ye visited me: I was in prison, and ye came unto me.* ³⁷*Then shall the righteous answer him, saying, Lord, when saw we thee an hungered, and fed thee? or thirsty, and gave thee drink?* ³⁸*When saw we thee a stranger, and took thee in? or naked, and clothed thee?* ³⁹*Or when saw we thee sick, or in prison, and came unto thee?* ⁴⁰*And the King shall answer and say unto them, Verily I say unto you, Inasmuch as ye have done it unto one of the least of these my brethren, ye have done it unto me.* ⁴¹*Then shall he say also unto them on the left hand, Depart from me, ye cursed, into everlasting fire, prepared for the devil and his angels:* ⁴²*For I was an hungered, and ye gave me no meat: I was thirsty, and ye gave me no drink:* ⁴³*I was a stranger, and ye took me not in: naked, and ye clothed me not: sick, and in prison, and ye visited me not.* ⁴⁴*Then shall they also answer him, saying, Lord, when saw we thee an hungered, or athirst, or a stranger, or naked, or sick, or in prison, and did not minister unto thee?* ⁴⁵*Then shall he answer them, saying, Verily I say unto you, Inasmuch as ye did it not to one of the least of these, ye did it not to me.* ⁴⁶*And these shall go away into everlasting punishment: but the righteous into life eternal.*" (Matthew 25:31-46)

This Bible passage under consideration is summarized as follows:

- The judgment of the nations is at the parousia (coming) of Christ.

- The judgment is after the great tribulation

- The judgment is on earth.

- All of the holy angels are present with Him.

- All of the nations (people) are the subjects of the judgment and are gathered before Him.

- He separates the sheep from the goats.

- The sheep helped Christ's "brethren" but had no knowledge of their doing so.

- The kingdom had been prepared ahead of time for the sheep.

- The sheep are righteous, or become righteous, and inherit eternal life.

- The goats did not help Christ's "brethren" at any time.

- The goats inherit everlasting punishment which is the fire that was prepared for Satan and his rebellious angels.

A surface reading would simply indicate that all the good guys go into the kingdom, and all the bad guys are cast into everlasting punishment at the time of Christ's coming; but such a simplistic evaluation contradicts other clear scripture (e.g. Zec. 14:16, etc.). The pre-tribulationists believe there are <u>no</u> unsaved people who enter the 1000 year kingdom, while the pre-wrath and post-tribulationists maintain that there are perhaps as many as one third of the worlds unsaved population who enter. The unsaved would be ruled over by the resurrected and glorified saints after the kingdom setup. It appears that the *"sheep"* in our text acquired their righteousness and favor by a <u>works</u>

based salvation, and the goats also received their punishment because of their lack of good works; therein lies a very real biblical dilemma. We know from the above scriptures, and many others, that salvation comes by the grace of God and not from our own works, and Hell is the result of rejection and unbelief in the atonement work of Jesus Christ. But let's step back for a moment and look at the larger picture of the events occurring after the close of the week, and then try to mesh our sheep and goat passage with them. A few of those events are:

- The 7 vial (bowl) judgments
- The battle of Armageddon (occurring within a 30 day period or less)
- The destruction of Babylon (false religions, The Roman Church, and all occults)
- The destruction of Antichrist and the false prophet
- The appearing of Jesus Christ
- A resurrection and rapture of all New and Old Testament saints
- The binding of Satan (by one angel)
- The New Jerusalem coming down from Heaven (our future home for all eternity)
- The rebuilding of the new Jerusalem temple
- Judgment of the sheep and the goats (vials and Armageddon)
- The marriage supper with Christ and all the saints

Jesus has said that He will come down from Heaven to gather His elect immediately after the great tribulation (Mt. 24:29-30) and that every living person will see Him coming (Rev. 1:7). We know also, that the sealed and protected Jews are fleeing to the valley of Azal just before the vials and Armageddon campaign (Zec. 14:4-5). We now come to the meshing part of our text. The goats in this judgment may very well be an equivalence to represent the ones who die with the dispersing of the vials and the battle of Armageddon. The subjects would also include those who took the mark and survived, but did harm to God's elect. The sheep on the other hand would include those who survive the tribulation without taking the mark and who helped the Christians and fleeing Jews. Obviously, the expression of the sheep and goats is symbolic in nature, so an analogy or an equivalence would be in order. These "sheep" will be those who have not heard the Gospel and will be amongst those who enter the kingdom to follow the ways of the Lord. To support such a thought of an equivalence, we see that God uses the exactly the same verbiage in the Old Testament when describing the battle of Armageddon, *"²I will also gather all nations, and will bring them down into the valley of Jehoshaphat, and will plead with them there for my people and for my heritage Israel, whom they have scattered among the nations, and parted my land. ¹²Let the heathen be wakened, and come up to the valley of Jehoshaphat: for there will I sit to judge all the heathen round about. ¹³Put ye in the sickle, for the harvest is ripe: come, get you down; for the press is full, the vats overflow; for their wickedness is great. ¹⁴Multitudes, multitudes in the valley of decision: for the day of the LORD is near in the valley of decision"* (Joel 3:2, 12-14). Here we see related language that Jesus used in the sheep and goat judgment. He is gathering the nations, judging the heathen, and sitting on His throne. These all refer to a physical battle. And to show again the equivalence in the New Testament we quote John, *"¹²And the sixth angel poured out his vial upon the great river Euphrates; and the water thereof was dried up, that the way of the kings of the east might be prepared.* [13]*And I saw three unclean spirits like frogs come out of the mouth of the dragon, and out of the mouth of the beast, and out of the mouth of the false prophet.* [14]*For they are the spirits of devils, working miracles, which go forth unto the kings of the earth and of the whole world, to gather them to the battle of that great day of God Almighty.* [15]*Behold, I come as a thief. Blessed is he that watcheth, and keepeth his garments, lest he walk naked, and they see his shame.* [16]*And he gathered them together into a place called in the Hebrew tongue Armageddon"* (Rev. 16:12-16). Here Satan, Antichrist, and the false prophet gathers the world armies together against Christ and His armies. This would be what Jesus said in our Matthew 25 text, where He gathers the nations of the world to judge. The sitting on the throne would represent His authority. Is it possible that when He came back with His saints and angels, that all of this judging and separating is taking place while we are all in the atmospheric heavens and watching from above?

Continuing our thoughts, there are a variety of unsaved people who are left at the close of the week. They would naturally include the following categories, which we will discuss one by one:

1) The leftover soldiers who fought against the armies of Christ and survived.

2) The women and children who were related to the soldiers who fought against Christ.

3) The people who took Antichrist's name, his number, and those who worshipped him (remember, the 1st vial punished them for taking the mark, but they did not die nec-

essarily, and may be sentenced at a later date, at the great white throne judgment).

4) The unsaved who didn't take the mark, who live in far off countries, and were not part of Antichrist's kingdom, and those who have never heard of Christ.

5) The unsaved who thought that they were saved, but didn't take the mark, but helped either the Jews or believers, or both.

Category "<u>one</u>" are the soldiers who fought against Christ and His armies at Armageddon. Zechariah tells us, *"And is shall come to pass, that <u>every one that is left of all the nations which came against Jerusalem,</u> shall even go up from year to year to worship the King, the Lord of hosts, and to keep the feast of tabernacles"* (Zec. 14:16). As we discussed before, God allows some of these people to live who were not in Antichrist's kingdom but were from far away nations. Micah asserted, as previously brought out, *"²And <u>many nations shall come,</u> and say, Come, and let us go up to the mountain of the LORD, and to the house of the God of Jacob; and he will teach us of his ways, and we will walk in his paths: for the law shall go forth of Zion, and the word of the LORD from Jerusalem. ³And he shall judge among many people, and rebuke strong nations afar off; and they shall beat their swords into plowshares, and their spears into pruning hooks: nation shall not lift up a sword against nation, neither shall they learn war any more. ⁴But they shall sit every man under his vine and under his fig tree; and none shall make them afraid: for the mouth of the LORD of hosts hath spoken it. ⁵For all people will walk every one in the name of his god, and we will walk in the name of the LORD our God for ever and ever"* (Micah 4:2-5). From this passage, it appears that the <u>unsaved</u> will learn about the ways of Christ at the beginning of the 1000 year kingdom. If there are no survivors who enter the kingdom, then where did these people come from? Some of these subjects are sheep and some of them are goats, obviously, the ones who continue to worship other gods, are goats, and will be judged at the end of the kingdom (Rev. 20:12-15).

We also know that with the first vial, God judges all of those who took the mark, for John says, *"¹And I heard a great voice out of the temple saying to the seven angels, Go your ways, and pour out the vials of the wrath of God upon the earth. ²And the <u>first</u> went, and poured out his vial upon the earth; and there fell a noisome and grievous sore upon the men which had the mark of the beast, and upon them which worshipped his image"* (Rev. 16:1-2). These would be goats and all who took the mark, and fought with Antichrist are destined for Hell. This first judgment takes place immediately after the close of the week, but all of these goats who took the mark are not necessarily killed upon entering the kingdom (as evidenced from the 1ˢᵗ vial), but their actual sentence could be carried out at the white throne judgment at the end of the 1000 years. During the kingdom, those and other sinners will die early. Isaiah said, in a millennial setting which all pre-millennial adherents agree on, *"There shall be no more thence an infant of days, nor an old man that hath not filled his days: for the child shall die an hundred years old; but <u>the sinner being an hundred years old shall be accursed</u>."* (Isa. 65:20). Here we see that the sinner does not necessarily die at 100 years old, but that he is accursed. That means he is destined for the lake of fire in the final end. Paul said, *"What if God, willing to show his wrath, and to make his power known, endured <u>with much longsuffering</u>*

the vessels of wrath fitted to destruction..." (Ro. 9:22). These
people probably will be serving the nation of Israel like Isaiah
indicated (Isa. 60:10-13).

Category "two" could possibly include the women and children around the world who were related to the soldiers who
fought against Christ and His armies at the end of the week.
Many of these wives, sons, daughters, grandmothers, grand-
fathers, etc. will survive because of their geographical location
in the world. When Christ comes back, some in this group will
have been judged by the various plagues and Armageddon
itself, but others including some expecting wives who didn't
take the mark, may become sheep; the rest are goats, who can
never become sheep. The goats will be raised for sentencing
at the end of the 1000 years in the *"resurrection of the unjust"*
(Acts 24:15; Rev. 20:4-15), also known as the *"second death"*
(Rev. 20:6). Even though the rapture has already taken place,
God's grace and love will never cease, because they are immu-
table attributes.

Category "three" people are the ones who surrendered
their soul to Satan by taking Antichrist's mark and worshipping his image. They did this to be able to purchase food, gas,
rations of sorts, and to survive physically, but at the expense of
their soul; they are goats. This was done against the clear warning of Christians as well as an angel of God. When John was
"in the spirit" on the *"Lord's day,"* (Rev. 1:10), he saw three
trumpet angels preaching the everlasting gospel to every living soul on earth. They cautioned people just before the start
of the great tribulation, *"⁶And I saw another angel fly in the
midst of heaven, having the everlasting gospel to preach unto
them that dwell on the earth, and to every nation, and kindred,
and tongue, and people, ⁷Saying with a loud voice, Fear God,*

and give glory to him; for <u>the hour of his judgment is come</u>: and worship him that made heaven, and earth, and the sea, and the fountains of waters. ⁸And there followed another angel, saying, Babylon is fallen, is fallen, that great city, because she made all nations drink of the wine of the wrath of her fornication. ⁹And the third angel followed them, saying with a loud voice, If any man worship the beast and his image, and receive his mark in his forehead, or in his hand, ¹⁰The same shall drink of the wine of the wrath of God, which is poured out without mixture into the cup of his indignation; and <u>he shall be tormented with fire and brimstone in the presence of the holy angels, and in the presence of the Lamb</u>: ¹¹and the smoke of their torment ascendeth up for ever and ever: and they have no rest day nor night, who worship the beast and his image, and whosever receiveth the mark of his name" (Rev. 14:5-11). With a warning like this, it is apparent that the ones that didn't heed it are goats and they will be judged and sentenced accordingly. Again, the actual sentence may not be carried out until the great "white throne judgment" at the end of the millennium (Rev. 20:12-15). This action would be much like a murderer being judged, found guilty, and sentenced to death; but the actual execution is not carried out until a later date.

In category "<u>four</u>" we have those people who never heard the Gospel, many of which may live in remote areas of the globe. They didn't take the mark because of their location with respect to the kingdom of Antichrist. There are people who live in places on earth who have never been seen by anyone, let alone had the Gospel declared to them. These people do not speak, read, or understand any other language or dialect but their own tribal ones, which may be entirely unknown to the rest of the world. Some of these will become sheep and some will become goats, all in accordance with election and the mercy and grace of God.

Finally, in category "<u>five</u>" are the people who didn't take the mark, or worship the image of Antichrist an helped either the Christians or Jews, or both during the hour of tribulation. They would be living in the vicinity of the Middle East, and more specifically, in the countries immediately surrounding Israel (but they could live anywhere on earth and be helping Christians and Jews). These may have been in liberal churches and never got saved. John tells us, *"¹And after these things I saw another angel come down from heaven, having great power; and the earth was lightened with his glory. ²And he cried mightily with a strong voice, saying, Babylon the great is fallen, is fallen, and is become the habitation of devils, and the hold of every foul spirit, and a cage of every unclean and hateful bird. ³For all nations have drunk of the wine of the wrath of her fornication, and the kings of the earth have committed fornication with her, and the merchants of the earth are waxed rich through the abundance of her delicacies. ⁴And I heard another voice from heaven, saying, <u>Come out of her, my people, that ye be not partakers of her sins, and that ye receive not of her plagues</u>"* (Rev. 18:1-4). These may be ones that thought they were saved, perhaps in Catholic Churches around the world, or in liberal churches but were deceived by their leaders. These will be part of the sheep who go into the kingdom to learn about the true Christ and His ways. They are His people because they were in the *"book of life"* from the foundation of the world and are of the elect (Rev. 13:8).

See, like I said, the sheep and goat judgment is not as easy as it first appears. Christ knows the hearts of individual people because they were in the book of life to begin with before the foundation of the world (Eph. 1:4; Rev. 13:18, 17:8). So, all of those in the book of life will be the sheep and all the rest will be goats. That's the way I feel that holy scriptures teach it. The *"overcomer"* will never be blotted out of the book. John said, *"He that overcometh, the same shall be clothed in white raiment; and I will not blot out his name out of the book of life, but I will confess his name before my Father, and before his angels"* (Rev. 3:5). John further describes the *"overcomer"* as one who has trusted Christ as his personal saviour by believing in His death, burial, and resurrection (I Jn. 5:5).

One thing is for sure – God's grace, love, and mercy is everlasting! Throughout the Bible we have examples of his compassion and grace upon whole nations and individuals as well. Paul made it plain about sovereignty when he recorded what God said to Isaiah, *"...¹⁵I will have mercy on whom I will have mercy, and I will have compassion on whom I will have compassion. ¹⁶So then it is not of him that willeth, nor of him that runneth, but of God that showeth mercy.* (Ro. 9:15-16). After the rapture and resurrection, things change and no one on this earth can say how, why, or who God has favor on.

(4) The Revealing of Antichrist and the Removal of the Holy Spirit

It is difficult to see why the placement of the "revealing" of Antichrist has become problematic. If you are of the pre-trib persuasion most of you will place the revealing at the beginning of the week. By definition, the word "reveal" means to expose, or to uncover something not previously known, such as a secret. So placing the "revealing" of the man of sin at the beginning of the week would mean that everyone would know what Antichrist was up to, or at least his identity. If he was revealed at the start of the week, the Jews would not enter into a covenant of peace with him or his allies. The leaders of Israel will enter a peace accord because of his deception, not because they know who he is, or what destruction he has planned - it will be a covenant of death! You cannot separate this "revealing" with what is associated with it. Paul said that when Antichrist is revealed, he will be sitting in the temple as God. And to do this, the invasion of Jerusalem would have to transpire. So, it appears to be that simple, it cannot be in the beginning of the week.

Hal Lindsey's places the revealing several literal weeks <u>before</u> the week even begins. Chart #7 is one that I have made, reflecting the one that he has in his book, entitled, *"The Rapture"* *p.167* (further quotes relevant to chart #7 will be found in Lindsey's same book.) I will use Mr. Lindsey, a fellow believer, as an example of the pre-trib position because he has influenced many believers through his written material, and not because there is any significant difference in his pre-trib viewpoint. There are a few comments that I will make about some of the events he has listed, and the timing of them. Notice first, that Lindsey has the rapture commencing "several weeks" before the peace covenant is signed as opposed to most pre-trib followers. One might ask what scripture shows, or alludes to the parousia of Christ in that time frame? And as we have pointed out, he places the "unveiling" and identification of Antichrist several weeks before the week begins. He says, *"The Roman dictator must be unveiled a short while before the actual beginning of Daniel's 70ᵗʰ week, which also <u>begins</u> the Day of the Lord"* (p.151). With that observation I would have to strongly disagree. If there was any prophetic passage of scripture that is made absolutely clear, it would be in II Thessalonians 2, where Paul talks about the man of sin being revealed; Paul states, *"³Let no man deceive you by any means: for <u>that day</u>* (day of the Lord) *shall not come, except there come a falling away first, and that man of sin be revealed, the son of perdition;* [4]*who opposeth and exalteth himself above all that is called God, or that is worshipped; so that <u>he as God sitteth in the temple of God, showing himself that he is God</u>"* (vs. 3-4). Antichrist doesn't do what is being described until the <u>middle</u> of the week (Dan. 9:27); that's what the ***"the abomination of desolation"*** is by its very essence. Lindsey agrees that the abomination is in the middle, but makes a distinction between that and the revealing, which he says is when the Antichrist will receive a deadly wound and then be healed. But if Antichrist did reveal himself as God to the world or to Israel at the start of the week, why would they sign a peace accord? According to Lindsey, it is the Antichrist (Roman dictator) and the <u>false prophet</u> who sign a treaty at the start of the week. He writes, *"When the Antichrist and the Israeli pseudo-Messiah sign the treaty of protection for Israel, the last seven years of Daniel's prophecy begins" (p.7).* He quotes Daniel 9:27 for his reference, but that is not really what that Daniel's text implies. The verse says, ***"And <u>he</u> shall confirm the covenant <u>with many</u> for one week…"*** Antichrist is dealing with *"many,"* not with the 2nd beast in Revelation 13, who we all refer to as the "false prophet." We must remember that most of the events in the 70th week of Daniel takes place <u>within</u> the 70th week, that's what Revelation is all about, at least chapters 6-19. It is apparent Lindsey concludes that the revealing of Antichrist and the abomination of desolation is somehow different. I believe that Antichrist is revealed when he abominates the temple! With regard to the abomination Lindsey states, *"he will take his throne into the holy of holies of the third Jewish temple which must be rebuilt upon its ancient site. This act will fulfill Daniel's and Jesus' prophecy concerning the "abomination of desolation" <u>which officially begins</u>*

the last three and one-half years of the tribulation period." (*There's a New World Coming" p.178);* but then he places the <u>revealing</u> several weeks before the beginning of what he believes is the 7 years of tribulation. It can't be both ways! Antichrist is revealed to the Jews when he invades Jerusalem with his armies and abominates the temple in the middle of the week; that's when they know they been had! Actually there is nothing in scripture that states that Antichrist even makes a treaty with Israel, but only that he *"confirms"* it after the treaty with *"the many"* is made (Dan. 9:27). It appears that Israel enters into a peace accord with *"many"* of the Arab countries, and that Antichrist agrees with it and signs it also. To "confirm," is like confirming a dentist appointment that has previously been made; it makes it sure. It could very well be, that with the new Palestinian state evolving, that a 7 year treaty between Israel and the Palestinians would be "confirmed" by 15-20 other Arab nations; thus, you would not know which one of the 15-20 signers is the Antichrist.

Lindsey also shows, in chart #7, the <u>removal</u> of the Holy Spirit several literal weeks before the 70th week begins, but yet maintains that the Holy Spirit will still convict millions of people during the tribulation. In his book, Lindsey again writes, *"The Holy Spirit will endow the 144,000 chosen Israelites with the same kind of power He did the prophets in the Old Testament. In fact, two of the mightiest prophets from the economy of law will return to shake up the world. The Holy Spirit will convince men of their need of salvation, bring them to faith and regenerate them as He did from the beginning of man's sin. But the unique Church economy ministries of <u>indwelling, baptizing, sealing, gifting and filling of every believer will be removed with the Church"</u>* (p.163). Here he is giving the "tribulation" Christians a "partial" power of the Holy

Spirit, kinda' like a car running on three cylinders instead of four. And in regards to the 144,000 Jews, *"They are apparently supernaturally converted just before, or at the very beginning of the tribulation much like the Apostle Paul...And since these are going to be men with a price on their heads, only a true believer will risk death to help them"* (p.173). Lindsey then says that the 144,000 can not die, and the great numberless multitude in Revelation 7, will be martyred to protect the evangelists from Antichrist. And concerning those who will survive, and those who won't, he says, *"Finally, with both the unbelieving Israelites and Gentiles removed in judgment, the Kingdom begins with only believers"* (p.174).

When you think about what Mr. Lindsey has said in the above statements, regarding the operation of the Holy Spirit in respect to the saints, it would seem that he has introduced a new method of salvation based upon their own works to make it through the week. When you take away the operation and special attributes of the Holy Spirit within the believer, what's left? Without the sealing of the Holy Spirit, Satan can have access to your soul! Gundry, a post-tribulation author, calls this a "reversal of Pentecost," and on that point I totally agree with him. How can we eradicate all of these believers promises, especially the sealing and filling of the Holy Spirit, and expect someone to become saved? Paul said, *"In whom ye also trusted, after that ye heard the word of truth, the gospel of your salvation: in whom* also *after that ye believed, ye were sealed with that holy Spirit of promise"* (Eph. 1:13). And again Paul declares, *"And grieve not the holy Spirit of God, whereby ye are sealed unto the day of redemption"* (Eph. 4:30). These verses are very clear! If these Christian saints are supposed to be led to the Lord by the supposed 144,000 Jewish witnesses, but don't have the sealing of the Holy Spirit, then we have a conflict in scripture. Paul clearly states that believers are sealed until the day of redemption and for the tribulation saints, that is not until the end of the week. Therefore they are called, saved, justified, sealed, and will have the same Holy Spirit's presence as we enjoy today! There would have to be some verse or passage in the Bible that indicates that the Holy Spirit won't indwell and seal the believer, or a passage indicating the method of salvation has reverted back to the days of Mosaic law to even remotely consider this bizarre assumption. Can you really imagine someone who wasn't sealed or indwelled with the Holy Spirit, making it through the great tribulation on their own? There is no genuine reason to remove the Spirit during the last week of mans history.

And while we are on the subject, where is the scripture that indicates that the 144,000 Jews are not physically able to die? It seems more apparent that the 144,000 were the converts of the two witnesses because they were *"first fruits unto God and the Lamb"* (Rev. 14:4), and are probably the surviving remnant who are fleeing to valley of Azal at the return of Christ to the Mount of Olives (Zec. 14:4-5). They were sealed in chapter 7 of Revelation to protect them from the various plagues that the world will encounter during the 2nd half of the week. There is nothing in scripture that assigns the role of witnessing to these 144,000 Jews, especially to the Gentiles; they are busy surviving another holocaust. And to suggest that the 144,000 in Revelation 14 are a different group than the 144,000 in Revelation 7, is unreasonable. If they were indeed different, John would have introduced them with an explanation earlier on in the text; God is not the author of confusion. Using the normal, natural exegetical approach demands them to be one and the same people, otherwise prophecy would be utterly hopeless and totally subjective.

(6) Elijah Comes Before the Day of the Lord

The very last prophecy in the Old Testament is in the book of Malachi. We read, *"Behold, I will send you <u>Elijah</u> the prophet <u>before</u> the coming of the great and dreadful <u>day of the Lord</u>..."* This is a very clear text confirming that Elijah comes sometime before that day, but it does not say how much before. Wherever you place the "rapture," the *"day of the Lord"* must immediately follow it. To this statement most pre-trib commentaries agree. This connection and observation is based on our rapture passage of I Thess. 4:16-18; 5:2, which says, *"¹⁶For the Lord himself shall descend from heaven with a shout, with the voice of the archangel, and with the trump of God: and the dead in Christ shall rise first: ¹⁷Then we which are alive and remain shall be caught up together with them in the clouds, to meet the Lord in the air: and so shall we ever be with the Lord. ¹⁸Wherefore comfort one another with these words. ⁵:¹<u>But</u> of the times and the seasons, brethren, ye have no need that I write unto you. ⁵:²For yourselves know perfectly that the <u>day of the Lord</u> so cometh as a thief in the night."* The conjunction *"but"* in verse one of chapter 5, is the rapture link to the *"day of the Lord."* We must ask ourselves, the *"times and the seasons"* of what? By normal interpretation, it would be the resurrection and rapture that Paul just described in the 5 previous verses, 14-18 of chapter 4. There is little doubt that the day of the Lord and the rapture go together. If the *"day of the Lord"* was placed at the beginning of the week, then the pre-trib people would have signs, because Elijah must physically show himself before that day and there must be cosmic events prior to that event

(Joel 2:10). When celebrating the Passover, today's Orthodox Jews set a symbolic place at the dinner table for Elijah to show their expectation of the fulfillment of Malachi 4:5. His coming will surely awaken the lost of Israel to salvation. For the Christians today, and as a side benefit, we are privileged to see the <u>Jewish</u> signs of the end times when they occur, just as in the days when Jerusalem was destroyed in 70 AD (as prophesied in Dan. 9:26), and again when they became a nation in 1948 and started the re-gathering back into their land. I believe that we shall also see the peace covenant made involving Israel and the many Arab nations, and that's when the real witnessing will begin. Christians will become serious in the task of witnessing as they enter the final 7 years and as the persecution becomes more intense.

(7) The "Last Day" and the Resurrection

If you place the *"coming"* of Christ at the beginning of the 70th week, you must also place the *"end of the world"* (age) there also; and if you place the *"end of the world"* there, then the *"last day"* must be with it as well. This is because our bodily resurrection is at the last day, and not just for the Jews as our text will show, but for Christians (saints) as well. We will list a few verses that use the phrase *"last day,"* in the context of prophecy, and then comment on them (not to be confused with the term *"last days"*).

When Jesus was talking to the multitude, he said, *"39And this is the Father's will which hath sent me, that of all which he hath given me I should lose nothing, but should raise it up again at the <u>last day</u>. 40And this is the will of him that sent me, that every one which seeth the Son, and believeth on him, may have everlasting life: and I will raise him up at the <u>last</u>*

day. ⁴⁴_No. man can come to me, except the Father which hath sent me draw him: and I will raise him up at the last day_ (Jn. 6:39-40, 44). Here we see Jesus making a statement exhorting the multitude on two things:

1) He is saying, in essence, that anyone who becomes a Christian, by believing on Jesus Christ, will have eternal life and will be resurrected on the _"last day."_

2) Nobody can become a Christian unless the Father draws him, and if He does, that person will be resurrected on the _"last day."_

And then again Jesus says, _"He that rejecteth me, and receiveth not my words, hath one that judgeth him: the word that I have spoken, the same shall judge him in the last day"_ (Jn. 12:48). This would seem to indicate, that whoever rejects the Saviour will not participate in the first resurrection, but will be resurrected for judgment after the 1000 years with the rest of the wicked and will experience the second death which true Christians will never experience. Whenever the _"last day"_ occurs, these living unbelievers will be judged by their absence in the _"first resurrection,"_ only to be held over until the "second" resurrection which is of the _"unjust"_ (Acts 24.15). In any of the preceding verses, there is no mention or hint of two phases of the _"last day,"_ nor is there a distinction between the so called "tribulation saints" and some other group of saints that allegedly disappeared 7 years earlier in a secret silent rapture; and besides this, Jesus said that the judgment is at the _"last day,"_ indicative of the end of the week, not the beginning. By the very nature of the definition of the word _"last,"_ it is final in a sequence of an order of things; more specifically, it will be when all the days of mans control of the earth have been concluded. We have already shown that the resurrection, judgment, and rewards are at the end of the week, and not at any other time (Rev. 11:18; I Tim. 4:8; Mt. 16:27, etc.).

In John, chapter 11, we have the story of the death and the burial of Lazarus. Martha thought that if Jesus had been there before Lazarus died, He could have healed him, which of course He could have; but Jesus replied, *"Thy brother shall rise again."* Martha then said, *"I know that he shall rise again in the <u>resurrection</u> at the <u>last day</u>."* Jesus again replied, *"I am the resurrection, and the life: he that believeth in me, though he were dead, yet shall he live"* (vs. 23-25). Again, we have: (a) the resurrection, (b) rewards, and (c) the last day, occurring at, or about the same time as the Jews and Christians; and that will be when Jesus comes with His holy angels (Mt. 16:27; I Pet. 5:4; I Cor. 15:53, etc.).

In the O.T. we have several passages that indicate that the resurrection takes place at the end of the tribulation or soon afterward. In the book of Job, the writer says, *"O that thou wouldest hide me in the grave, that thou wouldest keep me secret, <u>until thy wrath be past,</u> that thou wouldest appoint me a set time, and remember me! If a man die, shall he live again? <u>all the days of my appointed time will I wait, till my change come</u>"* (14:13-14). Job had advanced knowledge of the mysteries of God through revelation or similar means. He knew that his body would be in the grave until God's intense wrath (great tribulation against Israel) was completed. Job also knew that at an appointed pre-ordained time he would experience a resurrection and a bodily change from the mortal to the immortal. We know also that he will have a glorified body because Elijah had one. Righteousness was imputed to the O.T. believers based upon their faith in Jehovah God, the same saving grace and faith that we have today. Paul said concerning that relationship of the O.T. saints, *"And were all baptized unto Moses in the cloud and in the sea; And did all eat the same spiritual meat; And did all drink the same spiritual drink: <u>for they drank of that spiritual Rock that followed them: and that Rock was Christ</u>.* (1 Cor. 10:2-4). The Jews that were deliberately blinded by God because of their unbelief will be grafted back into the original Olive tree at the end of the week (Ro. 11:24). They will live eternally in mortal bodies sustained by the trees of life along the river flowing from Jerusalem to the Dead Sea (Isa. 65:17-25; Ezek. 47:12). The wicked Jews, which would include some of the Pharisee's and Sadducee's, will be resurrected and go into shame and everlasting contempt (Hell – Lk. 16:19-31; Dan. 12:2).

Then we have king David who also knew about this marvelous change; he declared, *"As for me, I will behold thy face in righteousness: <u>I shall be satisfied, when I awake, with thy likeness</u>"* (Psalms 17:15). He was looking forward to a day when he would be raised out of the grave and become like Jesus Christ. In the New Testament, that statement would agree with John, *"Beloved, now we are children of God; and it has not yet been revealed what we shall be, but we know that when He is revealed, <u>we shall be like Him</u>, for we shall see Him as He is"* (I John 3:2 - this is a verse also showing the interchangeability of the words "coming" and "revealing" in reference to Christ's return). Paul also testified of the believers change, from the mortal to the immortal, when he declared, *"Behold, I show you a mystery; we shall not all sleep, but we shall <u>all</u> be changed, in a moment, in the twinkling of an eye, at the last trump: for the trumpet shall sound, and the dead shall be raised incor-*

ruptible, and we shall be changed" (I Cor. 15:51-52). Notice that Paul said that we shall <u>all</u> be changed, and that includes the saints in the tribulation period also; again we see evidence that there is no "special" operation of the Holy Spirit during the tribulation, nor is there a special group of Gentile saints who remain mortal after the rapture, which is professed by most pre-tribbers to take place at the start of the week, once again, unthinkable.

And for a last example of the resurrection at the *"last day,"* I shall use Isaiah. This prophet wrote more profusely about the future of Israel, than any other prophet of God. The great book of Isaiah is a gold mine of prophecy. He told us of a time that Jesus would come out of Heaven to punish the wicked people and then raise the dead. We read of this incredible prophecy, still very pertinent today, *"*<u>*¹⁹Thy dead men shall live, together with my dead body shall they arise*</u>*. Awake and sing, ye that dwell in dust: for thy dew is as the dew of herbs, and the earth shall cast out the dead. ²⁰Come, my people, enter thou into thy chambers, and shut thy doors about thee:* <u>*hide thyself as it were for a little moment, until the indignation be overpast*</u>*. ²¹For, behold, the LORD cometh out of his place to punish the inhabitants of the earth for their iniquity: the earth also shall disclose her blood, and shall no more cover her slain."* (Isa. 19-21).

The *"wrath"* and *"indignation"* that these godly prophets were talking about was the great tribulation – the time of Jacob's trouble (Jer. 30:31). They could see that they were going to be raised <u>after</u> that period, and not before. Jesus connected together: the Church, the resurrection, and the *"last day,"* thus placing the rapture of the saints at the end of the week. And when we couple the previous evidence with Acts 3:20-21, *"²⁰And he shall send Jesus Christ, which before was preached unto you:* <u>*²¹Whom the heaven must receive until the times of*</u> <u>*restitution of all things,*</u>*"* we see that Jesus remains in Heaven, until the time of restitution of all things, which again, is not at the beginning of the week, but rather at the end or shortly thereafter.

(8) Two Witnesses Start Their Ministry (REV. 11:1-6)

Another event, which appears to <u>start</u> at the middle of the week, or thereabouts, is the commencing of the ministry of God's two witnesses mentioned in Revelation, chapter 11. For now, we will discuss their biblical mission, identity, and powers. Let's quote the verses, and then briefly discuss them:

> *"¹And there was given unto me a reed like unto a rod: and the angel stood, saying, Rise and measure the temple of God, and the altar, and them that worship therein. ²But the court which is without the temple, leave out, and measure it not; for it is given unto the Gentiles: and the holy city shall they tread under foot forty and two months. ³And I will give power unto my two witnesses, and they shall prophesy a thousand two hundred and threescore days, clothed in sackcloth: ⁴These are the two olive trees, and the two candlesticks standing before the God of the earth. ⁵And if any man will hurt them, fire proceedeth out of their mouth, and devoureth their enemies: and if any man will hurt them, he must in this manner be killed. ⁶These have the power to shut heaven, that it rain not in the days of their prophecy: and have power to smite the earth with all plagues, as often as they will." (Rev. 11:1-6).*

Who are these two people? – The Bible simply doesn't say! Any identification by anyone, in any book or commentary (such as this), is pure supposition or conjecture. Our text does not even hint that these two are Old Testament saints, let alone reveal their proper names. Most of the commentaries that I have read with a pre-tribulational view, identify Elijah and Moses, or Enoch and Elijah as the two prophets. Their reasoning is as follows:

Moses exhibited many (but not all) of the powers described in the text, when executing the plagues upon Egypt (Ex. 7-10). And we find also, that Satan disputed with Michael, the archangel, about the body of Moses (Jude 9), Therefore, one of the witnesses is probably Moses.

Concerning Elijah, he was translated into Heaven by God, and never saw death (II Kings 2:11). The Bible says that it is appointed unto man **"once to die"** (Heb. 9:28). Elijah will come back to earth to experience death. And then also, the prophet Malachi promised that Elijah would return before the great and terrible **"day of the Lord"** (Mal. 4:5). therefore, Elijah must be the other witness. Another point for their identification as being Moses and Elijah, was their appearance with Jesus on the mount of transfiguration (Matt. 17). It is believed that this was a "sampling" of what our glorified bodies would be like, and these two are probably the same two as in Revelation. There is another contender for the position, and that would be Enoch. In Genesis, we find that he was suddenly removed from the earth, *"and he was not, for God took him"* (Gen. 25:24).

When you get right down to it, there is just as much scriptural evidence for conjecture, that John, the author of Revelation, could be one of the two also. In the verse immediately prior to the first verse of our text, we find the words of the angel to John, **"Thou must prophesy again before many peoples, and nations, and tongues, and kings"** (Rev. 10:11). What exactly does this phrase mean? Some older prominent scholarly men feel this verse is linked to the preceding one, where the angel hands John the **"little book,"** telling him to **"eat it up,"** and it that it would make his belly bitter, but in his mouth it would be taste sweet. This, they say, was symbolic of the reformation period, where John, taking the **"little book,"** represents the Church receiving the Bible once again (sweet), but had to be born with much tribulation (bitter). The "prophesying," of John could be the penning of the Gospel of the book of Revelation for all future generations of believers. That's another opinion. But, there are also those who interpret this *"prophesying again"* to be that of John returning as one of the two witnesses who will have angelic powers and will preach the **"Gospel of the kingdom"** during the 70th week. Do we have any written historical evidence that this portion of Scripture was actually fulfilled? Does Church history recording John leaving the Island of Patmos and witnessing to **"many peoples and nations, and tongues, and kings?"** I haven't read anything concerning the historical fulfillment of this prophecy! Others believe this to be John completing the rest of the book of Revelation --- which I am more inclined to agree to. John's witness to the nations, kings, and people of different languages via the Bible has certainly come to pass.

I would like to take the liberty of rendering my own possibility of who these two are (assuming one is not John). Upon closer examination, we find these **"two witnesses"** (v. 3) to be very special and powerful beings. They are plainly described as the **"two prophets"** (v. 10). In Matthew, chapter 17, and in Luke, chapter 9, we have the record of the "transfiguration" of Jesus, and the glorified appearances of Moses and Elijah before the apostles Peter, James, and John. These apostles actually saw the two prophets, **"who appeared in Glory"** (Luke 9:31), and looked upon them in their glorified bodies. It would be difficult for me to imagine that Moses and Elijah would revert back into their natural bodies (if that were possible) just so they could be killed again in human form. I realize that Elijah was translated and never saw death, but that doesn't negate the fact that he already has a glorified body as the Word records! And if they did not appear in "glorified" bodies, then the Apostles must have witnessed the appearance of "glorified" souls! (remember, flesh and blood cannot enter Heaven – 1 Cor. 15:50). Let us view some other portions of the Word that may shed light on who they could be.

The Two Olive Trees and the Two Candlesticks (Rev. 11:4)

Let us examine a biblical setting with minimal speculation. John records of these two witnesses, saying, **"These are <u>the</u> two olive trees and <u>the</u> two candlesticks standing before the God of the earth"** (11:4). Here we have a definite article **"the"** before the phrases **"two olive trees,"** and **"two candlesticks"** suggesting someone that God has previously reflected upon, or pre-ordained in scripture. I believe the two olive trees and the two candlesticks, mentioned in this passage, are the same types described by the prophet, Zechariah. In chapter 4, of Zechariah, we have a description of the success of Zerubbabel by the power of God. Concerning the construction of the foundation of the temple, God said, it would be accomplished, **"not by might, nor by power, but by my spirit, saith the Lord of hosts"** (v. 6b). This was in response to the question, **"what are these two olive trees?"** And later on, when asked who are these two olive trees and the two candlesticks, the angel answered Zechariah and declared, **"These are <u>the</u> two anointed**

ones, that stand by the Lord of the whole earth" (v. 14). These two **"anointed ones"** appear to be the same types found in chapter 6, of Zechariah. We have the same identical language, suggesting they are indeed, angels of God. In that chapter, we have four horses, symbolic of the four spirits of Heaven. Our text reads, **"These are the four spirits of the heavens, which go forth from standing before the Lord of all the earth"** (Zech. 6:5b). So, it would appear, the two **"anointed ones,"** in Zechariah, chapter four (the two olive trees and candlesticks which **"stand before the Lord"**), are the same two **"spirits"** in chapter six of Zechariah, and could be the same two witnesses in our Revelation text who also **"stand before God."** These angelic beings perform the functions of judgment and that of being messengers for God, and would certainly be consistent with other examples in the Word appertaining to the performance of angelic beings. In Revelation, chapter 14, we have another clue that possibly make these two witnesses angelic beings. During the reign of Antichrist, and the wrath of God, we have two angels coming down from Heaven, one of which will preach the **"everlasting Gospel"** (v. 6), and the other will be warning the inhabitants of the earth, not to take the mark, name or number of the beast (v. 9-10). The time period of both Revelation chapters 11, and 14, are both in perfect harmony for the time period in question: the second half of the week! We also discover that God, through angels, is "plaguing" the world in judgment for their rejection of the Gospel. We are told our **"two witnesses"** are also given the same angelic powers, **"to smite the earth with all plagues, as often as they will"** (11:6b). Not even Moses or Elijah had these tremendous powers, but were limited to both God's permission, the exact type of judgment, and a limited geographical area in Northern Africa. These witnesses have power over all of the earth and **"tormented"** the earth dwellers (11:10). Judgments of this magnitude are generally reserved and assigned to angels.

And lastly, concerning these **"two witnesses"** (who do appear to be angelic or angelic type beings), they could not be destroyed during the term of their ministry. When the two angels came into Sodom and Gomorrah to destroy it (Gen. 19), they both appeared in human form; they ate food (v.3); and they warned the people of an imminent judgment (v. 12-13). In another example of angels taking on fleshly human form, is found in the book of Judges chapter 6. In this instance, the angel of God materialized himself, sat under an oak tree, and then, with the appearance of a normal man, gave Gideon his orders from God. But, looking like a human, Gideon needed proof that he really was an angel of the Lord. Gideon then prepared a lunch, which the angel consumed by fire by touching it with his staff, and then he simply disappeared (needless to say Gideon was convinced a real angel of God had visited him). Abraham also had angels appear in human form and they both ate together.

I believe that God will allow these two witnesses to take on the same type of human form, judge the earth, and then allow them to be killed; and with absolutely no difficulty, God will raise them up, just as He did Jesus. This will be done in full view of all who are in Jerusalem, as well as those watching television, or viewing the scene on their cell phone. Can a spiritual body that is manifested in the flesh be killed? Wasn't Jesus a spiritual body manifested in flesh? Didn't He die a physical death?

Closing out these challenging thoughts about the two witnesses, I certainly would not be dogmatic in my viewpoint, that is, that they are angelic beings! And I'm not saying these two beings couldn't be Moses, Elijah, or Enoch (even though there is no real hard evidence): but if they are, they would already have glorified bodies (by the nature that Heaven cannot possess "flesh and blood" – I Cor. 15:50). Also, I feel the material presented here, is far more biblically orientated, than many other commentaries have presented; and not just pure conjecture! I feel the emphasis concerning their identity, was on the phrase, **"These are <u>the two olive trees</u>, and _the two candlesticks_ standing before the God of the earth."** It is always easy to repeat what others have said, but is it biblical? We must however, allow freedom of thought because we presently see through the glass "dimly." Paul said, _"For <u>now</u> we see through a glass, darkly, but then..."_ (I Cor. 13:12).

To sum up our thoughts concerning the identity of the two "witnesses," we find that they were connected to the performance of miracles, judgments, and plagues upon the unbelieving world. We also concluded that they could be powerful angelic or angelic type beings, but they could <u>not</u> be absolutely identified. We agreed also, that they could be Old Testament prophets in glorified bodies capable of being killed in the same earthly manner that Jesus was. The transfigured saints, Moses, Enoch, and Elijah, are contenders also because God calls His two witnesses, the _"two prophets."_

(9) (10) The Last Trumpet and the 7th Trumpet

"⁵¹Behold, I show you a mystery; We shall not all sleep, but we shall all be changed, ⁵²In a moment, in the twinkling of an eye, <u>at the last trump</u>: for the trumpet shall sound, and <u>the dead shall be raised</u> incorruptible, and we shall be changed. ⁵³For this corruptible must put on incorruption, and this mor-

tal must put on immortality" (I Cor. 15: 51-53). Paul tells us in this resurrection passage, that we will all be changed at the last trumpet. His statement implies that there were other trumpets prior to this one, and that this is the last in a series, with none to follow – last is last! By natural thought, this event could not happen in the beginning of the week because there must be a first trumpet somewhere, which would mean several signs before the rapture, and in addition, they would have to be placed outside the week, defeating the whole idea of containing the trumpets within the 70ᵗʰ week.

There are 3 thoughts about placing the *"last trumpet"* at the beginning of the week that appear to conflict with a pre-tribulation rapture position:

First, a description of the *"last trumpet"* does not appear to fit anywhere but at the end of the week. When it sounds, Christ takes over and readies the planet for His wrath. This is what John stated about the last trumpet, *"⁷But in the days of the voice of the <u>seventh</u> (last trumpet) <u>angel,</u> when he shall begin to sound, the mystery of God should be finished, as he hath declared to his servants the prophets. ¹¹:¹⁵And the <u>seventh </u>(trumpet) <u>angel sounded;</u> and there were great voices in heaven, saying, The kingdoms of this world are become the kingdoms of our Lord, and of his Christ; and he shall reign for ever and ever...¹⁷ᵇ thou hast taken to thee thy great power, and hast reigned...¹⁸and the nations were angry, and thy wrath is come, and the <u>time of the dead, that they should be judged,</u> and that thou shouldest give reward unto thy servants the prophets, and to the <u>saints,</u> and them that fear thy name, small and great; and shouldest destroy them which destroy the earth"* (Rev. 10:7; 11:15, 17b, 18). After reading this, we have several disclosures about the 7ᵗʰ and last trumpet:

- The mystery of God will be finished (the resurrection mystery in I Cor. 15:51).

- Christ has taken power and total control of all kingdoms.

- The nations were very angry (because of the previous 6 trumpets and seals).

- God's wrath is imminent (the 7 vials, which is the 3rd woe, and Armageddon).

- The resurrection is imminent (the first resurrection of Rev. 20:4, Dan 12:2, etc).

- Rewards given out to the O.T. prophets, the saints (the Church), and to all that fear God.

- A destruction is imminent for the wicked who destroy the earth (Armageddon, 7 vials).

At the sounding of the 7th and last trumpet, there will be no more! This is the time that all of God's people will be rewarded. This is the time of Christ's appearing! This is the time of the resurrection of the saints! While Paul is facing imminent death, he tells Timothy, *"¹I charge thee therefore before God, and the Lord Jesus Christ, who shall judge the quick (living) and the dead at his appearing and his kingdom…⁸I have fought a good fight, I have finished my course, I have kept the faith: Henceforth there is laid up for me a crown of righteousness, which the Lord, the righteous judge, shall give me at that day* (day of His appearing and kingdom – v.1) *and not to me only, but unto all them also that love his appearing"* (II Tim. 4:1, 8). Notice Paul connects the time of rewards to the beginning of Christ's kingdom and His appearing. This is a scene at the end of the week, with the sounding of the 7th trumpet! The idea of these events occurring 7 years earlier (the beginning of the week) is nowhere in sight; and the teaching that the 7th trumpet is different than the I Thessalonians 4 trumpet, or the I Corinthians 15 trumpet, does not hold water. Paul wrote about the rapture trumpet about 50 A.D. and then the resurrection trumpet in about 57 A.D.. So, when John, in about 90 A.D. wrote about the 7th trumpet in Revelation in all likelihood it was the same as Paul's. John just gave us more detail about that trumpet.

Second, The Church experiences a resurrection at the *"last trumpet"* (I Cor. 15:51). If you place the rapture at the beginning of the week, that's also where the *"last trumpet"* must occur. If the *"7th trumpet"* is not the same as the *"last trump,"* and the *"last trump"* is placed at the beginning, then who is it in Rev. 11:18, that is rising from the dead at the 7th trumpet? Again, this is another weak spot in the pre-trib position. Christ's "coming," "appearing" and "revealing" demands placement at the end of the week, occurring <u>immediately after</u> the great tribulation (Mt. 24:29-31). Once again, to dismiss Paul's *"last trump"* in Corinthians, and suggest that it is not the same as John's 7th and final trump, may be a bit shortsighted in light of the evidence.

Third, In Rev. 20:4-5, we have a picture of the <u>first resurrection</u> taking place. The saints (Church) have passed through the tribulation and John says, *"⁴And I saw thrones, and they sat upon them, and judgment was given unto them: and I saw the souls of them that were beheaded <u>for the witness of Jesus,</u> and for the word of God, and which had not worshipped the beast, neither his image, neither had received his mark upon their foreheads, or in their hands; and they lived and reigned with Christ a thousand years. ⁵But the rest of the dead lived not again until the thousand years were finished. <u>This is the first resurrection.</u>"* John's vision here, is one where some of the saints were beheaded for the witness of Jesus, and didn't capitulate to Antichrist. These saints were raised from the dead after the 7th trumpet sounded, they were given rewards, and they reigned with Christ; this is the first resurrection. How can the first resurrection take place at the beginning of the week if it is clear in this passage that it is at the end of the great tribulation? And, the fact that they will reign with Christ for all of the 1000 year period, suggests that there are unsaved people to reign over right from the very beginning of the 1000 years, as previously discussed.

Conclusion and Evaluation

We set out to demonstrate that there is only one coming (parousia) of Christ, and that Jesus said that it occurs immediately after the great tribulation which would be at the end of the 70th week. We also have shown, which I believe to be beyond a reasonable doubt, that there are too many conflicting passages of scripture to support another *"coming"* or "parousia" in the beginning of the week. It was shown, that the idea of an imminent return of Christ was unrealistic when confronted with conflicting scriptures, but we can be expecting His soon return, based on recent fulfilled Jewish signs that have already taken place (e.g.- Israel established as a nation, Jerusalem once again their capital, etc.). We concluded that the 70th week is imminent, based upon the re-gathering and the re-capturing of Jerusalem, and thus the 2nd advent.

I have constructed a post-tribulational chart (#8), showing what I feel the scriptures most confidently teach when all of the many passages are harmonized and with proper application of hermeneutics. I have quoted Tim Warner's (website: www.lasttrumpet.com) description and definition of the post-tribulation parousia, which reflects a portion, but certainly not all, of my personal beliefs as he writes in this context:

"The 'post-tribulation' rapture view is the belief that Jesus will return visibly and bodily to raise the dead Christians and gather together the living Christians at the end of a period of intense tribulation, called by Jesus 'great tribulation' (Matt. 24:21). The post-trib view is the only rapture view which sees only a single future coming of Jesus. All other rapture views, pre-trib, mid-trib, and pre-wrath, see the rapture and resurrection prior to the second coming of Jesus by months or years. While these rapture views see the rapture as a means to take the Church to heaven to escape God's wrath, the post-trib view sees the rapture as a mechanism to gather together believers from both heaven and earth in a single location with Christ, to be revealed with Him in glory to the world at His coming. Therefore, in a post-trib scenario, the rapture is an integral part of the second coming. Upon Jesus' descent from heaven, the angels will be dispatched by the trumpet blast and gather together Jesus' elect to meet Him in the air. Then the whole gathering of angels and saints are revealed to the world along with Jesus in a blaze of glory."

There are a great many additional events which occur beyond the 70th week which God has not yet chosen to reveal their exact timing. Many of those take place within the 75 days immediately following the great tribulation. Remember, the angel told Daniel to **"Go thy way, Daniel: for the words are closed up and sealed <u>until</u> the time of the end"** (Dan. 12:9). As we get closer to the final time of His coming, the Holy Spirit will uncover more veiled details relating to prophecy; meanwhile, we are to be about the Master's business and always ready to give an answer to anyone who asks about the hope that lies within us.

I have shared with you, my personal convictions and analysis of the parousia of Christ. I pray it will encourage you to re-evaluate the pre-tribulation position if you hold to such a view. Comments and suggestion are always welcomed; I certainly don't claim to have all of the answers by any means, but I do try to use as many <u>scriptures</u> that I can for the basis of my exposition, and not run on a path just because it is well traveled and easy going. But one thing for certain, I will have lot's of questions to ask my Saviour when I see Him face to face, and I'm sure there will be others standing in line behind me. But until then, let us enjoy a wonderful, but sometimes puzzling, excursion through the pages of timeless Truth.

I pray that this short study will be another point of light to the study of the second advent of Jesus Christ.

Glossary / Dictionary

(From a pre-millennial viewpoint)

ABOMINATION OF DESOLATION - This term is a quote from Jesus when warning his disciples about Antichrist and the desecration of the future temple that is yet to be built (futurist perspective). His warning is a quote from the book of Daniel in the Old Testament. It will be a future time when Antichrist desecrates the temple in Jerusalem, during the middle of the 70th week, and places an image in the temple to be worshipped by everyone in his kingdom. Those who will not worship the image will be subject to death (Matthew 24:15; Daniel 11:31, 12:11; Rev 13:14-15).

AMILLENNIAL RETURN OF CHRIST - A belief that there will not be a literal great tribulation period for the Jews or anyone else, nor is there coming a literal 1000 year reign of Christ on this earth. Adherents believe the kingdom of God is present in the Church age, which some call "realized millennialism" (so as not to deny a millennial period); however they do not deny the return of Christ. Rev. 20:4-6 would be viewed as the dead saints who are now reigning with Christ from Heaven. The kingdom of God is now present, and will be perfected when Christ returns and creates a new earth at the close of the age. Like post-millennialists, they believe the Church is the "new Israel" and there is no distinction between the two. At the end of this age, they see Christ coming again, bodily, visibly and personally, to raise all believers and unbelievers, at the same time, to be judged accordingly (same belief as post-millennialists). After this, the eternal state of all things will take place. They believe there will be many signs (like the pre-wrath and post-trib positions) before Christ's parousia, some of which would be: cosmic events, satanic miracles, the exposing of Antichrist, and the conversion of the remnant of Israel (they do not hold to a national conversion of Israel). What futurists of all positions view as literal in Revelation, amillennialists see as allegorical (chart #1).

ANTICHRIST - This is a reference to I John 2:18, and refers to an end time person who will be indwelled by the power of Satan much like Judas was. He will confirm a peace covenant with many Arab nations at the beginning of the 70th week (Daniel 9:27). His reign and power over the saints will be for 42 months during the "great tribulation," making Jerusalem to become desolate by his invading armies (Luke 21:20; Revelation 13:5). He is the "beast" in Revelation 13, and the "little horn" in Daniel 7. He is destroyed and cast into the lake of fire at the coming of Christ, along with the false prophet (II Thessalonians 2:8; Rev. 19:20).

APPEARING OF CHRIST - The meaning of this term depends upon your viewpoint. The appearing (epiphaneia), coming (parousia), and revealing (apokalupsis) are all one and the same if you view Christ's return as a one time single event.

If you are of the pre-tribulation persuasion, you see two "comings" or phases of Christ 7 years earlier than His "appearing" or His "revealing."

ARMAGEDDON - A final physical and spiritual battle between the armies of Antichrist and the armies of Christ. All rapture positions agree that the battle occurs sometime after the close of the 70th week. The only direct usage of the word occurs in Revelation 16:16. The effects of the battle are mentioned in Zechariah 14:12, and numerous other places in scripture. It is the absolute undiluted wrath of God being poured out upon unbelievers. It will most likely take place in the valley of Megiddo, located on the South rim of the plain of Esdraelon (about 50 miles North of Jerusalem), which was the scene of many decisive battles in the Old Testament.

BEAST, THE - In prophecy, a beast can represent various kingdoms in history (Daniel 7), or can represent a person. In Revelation 13:1, the *"beast that rises out of the sea,"* is Antichrist, and in Daniel, chapter 7 and 8, he is the "little horn," while in II Thessalonians 2, he is the "man of sin" and the "son of perdition." He derives his powers from Satan and will have power over the saints during the great tribulation. This beast is not to be confused with the 2nd beast who is the "false prophet" described in Revelation 13:11.

COMING OF CHRIST, THE - The word "coming," is derived, from the Greek term "parousia," (par-oo-see'-ah), and is used when referring to the advent of Jesus Christ. It simply means "presence" or "arrival." It is used in the "rapture" text of I Thessalonians 4:15, and all others pertaining to His "coming." The Greek word was used to describe the arrival of an important person and his entourage approaching a city, in which the city's delegation would go out and meet them, and escort them back into the city (see also "pre-tribulation rapture," "pre-wrath rapture," "mid-tribulation rapture," and "post-tribulation rapture" (chart #3 is agreed upon by all regarding the 2ⁿᵈ advent).

COSMIC EVENTS - In relation to our study, these are a specific set of celestial events occurring at the coming (parousia) of Christ. They affect the sun, moon, stars, and other heavenly forces, and introduce the wrath of God. They are described by Jesus (Matthew 24:29), John (Revelation 6:12-17), and Joel (Joel 2:1-11, 30-31), and are the same, and not separate events happening at different times. They occur: (1) at the 6ᵗʰ seal, (2) after the great tribulation, (3) before the day of the Lord, and (4) at the coming of Jesus Christ. Because Jesus describes these events as occurring immediately prior to His coming after the great tribulation, the believers will not be subject to the wrath of God. The 6ᵗʰ seal is the first mention of that wrath, therefore, the 6ᵗʰ seal must be immediately after the tribulation and at the start of the day of the Lord. The author sees the 7 vials and Armageddon as the wrath of God (see "Day of the Lord" and charts #10-15).

DAY OF THE LORD - A phrase that is mentioned over 20 times in the Bible, and a phrase never describing a good time. It is the time of the undiluted wrath of God poured out upon unbelievers. It consists of the 7 vials and Armageddon. The wrath of God is never directed at believers and they are spared from it (I Thessalonians 5:9). Most pre-trib books that I have read, see this day as starting at the beginning of the 70ᵗʰ week, and lasting until the end of the 1000 year period.

Many post-tribbers see it as a short period of God's wrath at the close of the 70th week, concluding with the battle of Armageddon. Pre-wrath followers see it as starting sometime in the 2nd half of the 70th week which would include the trumpets, vials, and the battle of Armageddon. It should be noted that there are variations within each position.

ELECT, THE - Again, that depends on your viewpoint. The pre-wrathers and post-tribbers, see all of the "elect" in the New Testament as the believing Church. The pre-tribbers also see the "elect" as the Church, except in Matthew 24; there they depart and make them Jewish only, thus affecting the view of the parousia of Christ. Pre-wrath and post-tribbers see that elect in the New Testament as the Church with no exceptions.

ELIJAH'S COMING - A reference to the future coming of Elijah the prophet before the day of the Lord (Malachi 4:5). If you view the day of the Lord starting at the beginning of the 70th week, which most pre-trib commentators do, then you will see the prophet as coming before that. If you view the day of the Lord as occurring at the end of the week, then Elijah comes sometime during the 70th week.

END OF THE WORLD - This is a phrase attributed to Jesus, when He said, *"...lo, I am with you always, even unto the end of the world."* And again when He said, *"So shall it be at the end of the world: the angels shall come forth, and sever the wicked from among the just."* (Mt. 13:49). The pre-trib adherents must place the end of the world at the beginning of the week because that is when they place the rapture and the removal of the Holy Spirit and the "just." Post-tribbers place it at the end of the week, and the pre-wrathers position it somewhere in the 2nd half until the end. Most commentators, with very few exceptions, see the rapture as immediately preceding the day of the Lord: in other words, wherever the rapture is placed, that's where the day of the Lord starts. The basis for this thinking is derived from the connection of the last verse in I Thessalonians 4, and the first verse in chapter 5. Paul is not introducing a new idea or topic, but is using the English word, *"but,"* as a transitional particle, or conjunction.

EXPECTANCY - This is a term used during the Niagara Bible Conference in the late 1800's and early 1900's. The term was used to replace the word imminency to better describe the coming of Christ for those who didn't view Christ's coming as an "any moment" event. The term, as used in prophecy, means that all necessary events could have been fulfilled in any person's lifetime before Christ returned; and any person born today can see the return of Christ and have the remaining signs fulfilled. In other words: Israel could have become a nation, re-captured Jerusalem, have the 70th week started, and rebuilt the temple in any persons lifetime in the past. This is what is meant by the term expectancy, and is the view of the author.

FALSE PROPHET - This is a title given to the "2nd beast" in Revelation 13:11. He causes people to create an image of the Antichrist, and then demands that all in Antichrist's kingdom worship the image. The false prophet has the power to kill anyone who does not worship it. He also has the same powers of Antichrist (as part of the unholy false Trinity), and can call down fire and perform miracles for the purpose of deceiving the people. He is destroyed by fire, along with Antichrist, at the return of Christ at the end of the week (Revelation 19:20).

FUTURIST - Opposed to Preterism and Historicism. A belief that most of the book of Revelation, and many prophetic portions of the Old Testament has yet to be fulfilled. In particular, they would be: (1) the 70th week of Daniel (2) a peace covenant between Israel and an alliance of Arab nations (3) a new Jewish temple (4) Elijah appearance again (5) the day of the Lord (6) the invasion of Jerusalem (7) the coming of Antichrist and the false prophet (8) the 1000 year literal kingdom (9) the bodily return of Christ (10) the bodily rapture and resurrection of all saints (11) the salvation of Israel (12) the binding and final destruction of Satan (13) the New Jerusalem coming down from Heaven (14) the restoration of all things, (and many more events).

GREAT MULTITUDE - This is taken from Revelation 7:9, in which John described a tremendous amount of Christians in Heaven. The verse in question says, *"After this I beheld, and, lo, a great multitude, which no man could number, of all nations, and kindreds, and people, and tongues, stood before the throne, and before the Lamb, clothed with white robes, and palms in their hands..."* There are two dissenting views on their identity: (1) The pre-tribbers see them as a group of believers who were converted by the 144,000 Jewish witnesses during the first half of the 70th week. (2) The pre-wrath and post-tribbers see them as the raptured Church. The latter positions both agree that they are the raptured Church, but differ as to when the event occurred. Post-trib sees the Church raptured at the end of the week and pre-wrath views the event as happening sometime in the 2nd half of the week.

HISTORICISM - There are 3 major views of prophecy: (1) Preterism, (2) Futurism, (3) Historicism. Historicism is a belief that the history of the Church is currently underway, and always present in the book of Revelation and parts of Daniel. Prophecy represents the time period from the 1st advent until the 2nd advent, in other words, Revelation and many of the prophecies in Daniel have been fulfilled. They believe that the Catholic Church (papacy) represents "Antichrist," also, the "man of sin," the "beast" in Revelation 13, and the "whore of Babylon." Historicists believe in the year-day theory, and view the specific time periods of: 3-1/2 years, 1260 days, 2300 days, 42 months, etc. as being years (e.g. - one day = 1 year), and thus have been fulfilled in past history. The Historicists main views would be: (1) the 70 weeks as being fulfilled in Judah's captivity in Babylon (2) the times of the Gentiles would be from the Babylonian captivity to the decline of Islam and the rise and restoration of Israel (3) the Jewish tribulation was from the fall of Jerusalem in 70 A.D until Israel is restored (4) the rise of papal Rome (Antichrist, or the beast), was from the late 5th century until Israel is restored (5) The return of Christ will be when Rome is destroyed, Israel restored, and then the 1000 (not literal) years begins.

IMMINENCY - Persons of the pre-trib persuasion use this term to describe the "rapture' event. They believe that Christ could come back at "any moment" in time, or at any previous time in the past since Pentecost. They also believe that there are no more signs to be fulfilled. Pre-wrath and post-tribbers view Christ's return with expectancy (see expectancy) and believe that more signs are necessary before the advent of Christ. Specifically, those signs will be: (1) the start of the 70th week (peace accord), (2) the re-building of the temple, (3) the abomination of desolation, (4) Elijah's appearance, and, (5) signs in the heavens (cosmic events).

LAST DAY, THE - This day is when the resurrected bodies of all believers are united with their souls. Jesus said, *"And this is the will of him that sent me, that every one which seeth the Son, and believeth on him, may have everlasting life: and I will raise him up at the last day."* Pre-tribbers must place the "last day" in the beginning of the week because that's where they place the rapture, which would include the resurrection. Pre-wrathers must see it sometime in the 2nd half of the week after the shortened tribulation. The post-tribbers see it at the end of the week. Basically, wherever you place the rapture, that's where the resurrection and the "last day" must be.

LAST DAYS - The "last days" engulf the time period from the death of Christ until He sets up His earthly kingdom. It is the last days because there is no more development in the manner of redemption. The cross was the only way for man to be redeemed by Christ's atonement. There is no other way for the unbeliever. The writer of Hebrews stated that they were living in the last days (Hebrews 1:2).

MAN OF SIN, THE - This phrase and title is taken from I Thessalonians 2:3. It is agreed that the phrase is the identification of Antichrist who will manifest himself during the middle of the 70th week. This "man of sin," is also called the "son of perdition" like the Apostle Judas was; the phrase "son of perdition" means to be utterly lost or destroyed (see Antichrist).

MID-TRIBULATION RAPTURE - This is a belief that the resurrection and rapture take place in the middle of the 70th week. Many who hold this view believe in a "partial" rapture with the faithful being removed before the great tribulation and the unfaithful believers left to go through it. The idea of mid-tribulation rapture, came from Norman Harrison in 1941 in his book, *"The End: Rethinking the Revelation."* Although he didn't name it that, others used the term which he accepted as accurate (chart #2).

NIAGARA BIBLE CONFERENCE - (1878-1909) This was an annual prophecy conference that re-defined and popularized pre-millennialism in North America. From the late 1790's to the mid 1870's, most pre-millennialists were "historic," who saw the bulk of Revelation and the prophecy parts of Daniel as being fulfilled in the current Church age, in many ways like the amillennialists of today. Although the participants of the Conference were pre-millennial, most were now seeing the 70th week of Daniel as future, with fulfillment of the week found in Revelation 6-19. In the beginning, the idea of "two comings" or "two phases" was not present, nor was there a dispensational tone in there doctrinal statement. Article 14, dealing with corporate eschatology, left out the rapture text of today (I Thess. 4:13-17), thus leaving room for all pre-millennialists, including historicists. Eventually, the teachings of John Darby permeated the conference and great debate took place over the idea of two comings or two phases of the parousia. Finally after the conference disbanded in 1909, the Sea-Cliff Bible conference took its place and its participants were totally dispensational and held to two parousia's with an "any moment" return. The funding for this start-up came from the Plymouth Brethren. This is the period where Scofield, Moody, Torrey, Gaebelein, Ironside,

Gray, and others advanced the idea of the imminent return of Christ. As a result, *"...the badge of North American evangelicalism was the Scofield Bible."* (This information was gleaned from Richard Reiter, co-author of *"The Rapture -Pre,-Mid,- or Post-Tribulational"* 1984, Zondervan, who did a fantastic job of documenting the advancement of the pre-millennial position. A further detailed study on the development of the various pre-millennial positions as written by Reiter, is highly recommended).

OLIVET DISCOURSE - A general reference to Matthew 24, when Jesus is talking to His disciples. It communicates both past and future events. The first part deals with the past destruction of Jerusalem in 70 A.D. (vs. 1-3) The mid-part (vs. 4-28) deals mostly with events leading up to and including the time of the great tribulation. The concluding part (vs. 29-31) details the 2nd advent of Christ with His angels and His gathering of the "elect." There is controversy in the different positions as to who the "elect" are, and whether their gathering is a picture of the rapture or not. Post-trib and pre-wrathers see the coming of Christ and the rapture as one event in every passage that relates to His return. Pre-trib people see the coming of Christ in this chapter, as well as others, as an event happening 7 years after the rapture which they believe to be at the beginning of the 70th week.

PAROUSIA - This is the Greek word for "coming" in prophecy. It is used by Paul in the rapture text of II Thessalonians 4, and by Jesus when He was teaching His disciples about His return to earth. Jesus declares that His parousia occurs "immediately after the great tribulation" (see also 'coming of Christ'). Pre-wrath adherents see the parousia as a continuing presence from the beginning of the shortened tribulation period until the end of the week. Pre-tribbers see two comings spaced 7 years apart, while post-tribbers see the parousia happening at the end of the week (chart #3 is a position that is agreed upon by all futurists). Note: Both pre-wrathers and Post-tribbers view the parousia as occurring after the great tribulation, but they see the length of the tribulation differently.

PARTIAL RAPTURE - A belief that only the faithful in Christ will be raptured before the great tribulation and the rest will be left to go through it. The faithful will be watching and waiting for the return of Christ. There are few that hold to such a position today.

POST-MILLENNIALISM - (not to be confused with post-tribulationalism). This was a widely held view by many theologians (especially in Europe) during the late nineteenth century, but there are many today that still hold this view. Generally, it is held that the kingdom of God is being built up right now, through the preaching and teaching of the Gospel. As a result of this action most of the world will become saved, thus ushering in the millennial kingdom (not a literal 1000 years) of eternal righteousness. The bodily, visible return of Christ will come as the result of this evangelistic effort and action. This is contrary to both the premillennial and amillennial views who see the world getting worse, not better, before the return of Christ. Concerning the end of mans history, they believe that Christ will come, and raise all of the righteous and the wicked, at the same time, commonly called a "general resurrection" which is based upon John 5:28-29. All people will be judged according to the deeds done in their body as well as their belief or disbelief in God's Son as the Saviour. The wicked will be consigned to the lake of fire, and the righteous will reside in Heaven, which will be the New Jerusalem City. Amillennialists are in agreement with the general resurrection, judgment, and the final disposition of souls.

POST-TRIBULATION RAPTURE - (not to be confused with post-millennialism). This is the belief that Christ will come once, and it will be at the end of the 70th week. The coming (parousia) of Christ will happen like Jesus said, *"But in those days, after that tribulation, the sun shall be darkened, and the moon shall not give her light, And the stars of heaven shall fall, and the powers that are in heaven shall be shaken. And then shall they see the Son of man coming in the clouds with great power and glory"* (Mark 13:24-26; Matthew 24:29-30). In light of what Jesus said, it would seem difficult to view the parousia at any other time unless there was clear mention of another in scripture. Post-tribulation is the belief and position held by the author (see also the "wrath of God," "cosmic events," and chart #8).

PRE-MILLENNIALISM (Dispensational) - This is the belief that Christ will come before the millennial kingdom, and will come for the purpose of setting it up. This is in fulfillment of many Old Testament prophecies to Israel for the Messiah to come as their Saviour and King. The positions of pre-tribulation, mid-tribulation, pre-wrath, and post-tribulation all hold to a pre-millennial return of Christ. The general position held by the early Church was pre-millennial, but not necessarily having dispensational characteristics which came much later during the early 19th century.

Within the pre-millennial camp, there are two types of beliefs; "historical" and "dispensational." The distinguishing beliefs of the "dispensational" view are: (1) that God has a separate program for Israel and the Church (2) the entire 70th week of Daniel is God's wrath called the tribulation period (3) the Church is removed from earth prior start of the 70th week (4) The Holy Spirit is also removed before the 70th week (5) the rewards of the saints are given out, in Heaven, prior to the 2nd advent (6) there are two comings (parousia's) or phases of Christ. (7) the rapture can come at "any moment" without signs, and will be secret and silent. (8) All of the unrighteous dead will be raised for judgment at the end of the literal 1000 years, at which time Hell, death are cast into the lake of fire. This form of pre-millennialism, in reference to Church history, is a new one, heavily propagated by the Plymouth Brethren in the early 1830's in England, and popularized in America in the early 20th century by Cyrus Scofield and other prominent theologians. A few of the popular theologians holding to this view, in general, are: Moody, Torrey, Gaebelein, Walvoord, Scofield, Gray, and Ironside. Although pre-wrath and post-tribbers are both pre-millennial, they part ways significantly with pre-tribulationalists on most aspects of eschatology (see chart #1).

PRE-MILLENNIALISM (Historical) - This is the belief that Christ will come before the millennial kingdom, and will come for the purpose of setting it up. This is in fulfillment of many Old Testament prophecies to Israel for the Messiah to come as their Saviour and King. All positions of pre-tribulation, mid-tribulation, pre-wrath, and post-tribulation hold to this viewpoint of a pre-millennial return of

Christ for those reasons. The general position held by the early Church was pre-millennial, but not necessarily having dispensational characteristics. Within the pre-millennial camp, there are two types of beliefs; "historical" and "dispensational." The distinguishing beliefs of the "<u>historic</u>" view are: (1) the Church would go through the entire 70th week (2) The wrath that the Church will suffer will be from the world and Satan (3) the Church would not suffer the wrath of God which is meted out upon unbelievers (4) there is only one coming (parousia) of Christ occurring just prior to the kingdom setup, and that the coming, appearing, and revelation are the same thing (5) the Old and New Testament saints are raised at the same time immediately prior to the establishment of Christ's kingdom (6) The rapture is not secret or silent and there will be signs before the parousia (7) Christ is reigning from Heaven now and will not just be reigning at the kingdom setup. He will continue to reign from a spiritual standpoint after the parousia for an unknown period of time, until He declares "the end" when He conquers Hell and death at which time the New Heavens and the New Earth are established. Two well known modern theologians holding to this view would be Barton Payne and George Ladd. Bear in mind that there are many modern variations within the "historic" and "dispensational" positions. Post-tribulationalists generally agree to this view, with the exception of #7 above (see chart #1).

<u>PRE-TRIBULATION RAPTURE</u> - This is the belief that Christ will come two times, or in two different phases. He will come at the beginning of the 70th week, and then again at the end of the week. A frequently used cliché is: He comes "for His saints" and then comes "with His saints." This teach-

ing originated in England as a defined position in the early 1800's, and very much popularized in the 20th century in America, especially through the Niagara Bible Conference (1878-1909), and notes in the Scofield Reference Bible (1917). It is taught that God has two separate programs for Israel and therefore the Church cannot be in the 70th week at the same time, thus bringing out one of the more specific teachings of dispensationalism. With this theory, Christ comes and gathers the living and the dead in Christ at the beginning of the week. Then, 144,000 supernaturally endowed Jewish witnesses convert millions and millions of Gentiles to Christ in the first half of the week. The "two witnesses" in Revelation 11, are also active during this time, but are killed at the mid-point of the 7 years. Some adherents have the trumpet judgments occurring in the first half, and others in the 2nd half of the week. All of the ones that were "left behind" after the rapture at the start of the week, will have a 2nd chance to become saved, but without the sealing or the indwelling of the Holy Spirit who was removed at the beginning of the week. All of these "new" converts will enter the kingdom in mortal bodies, and will reproduce; some of their offspring will be the ones who come up against Christ at the end of the 1000 years. They teach that no unbelievers will enter the kingdom period (charts #2, 4, 5).

PRE-WRATH RAPTURE - A rapture position advanced by Marvin Rosenthal in a book called *"The Pre-wrath Rapture of the Church,"* first published in 1990. Rosenthal was previously a strong "pre-tribulation" adherent for over 35 years, and a major player in pre-trib Bible conferences, and Editor and publisher of "Israel My Glory" a magazine reaching 35,000 pastors. Rosenthal changed positions, when confronted by a friend, with questions that could not be answered by the pre-trib rapture theory. His position teaches that the rapture will take place sometime in the 2nd half of the week, immediately after the "shortened" tribulation, at the cosmic events, and at an unknown time. He includes the trumpets, the vials, and Armageddon as the "wrath" of God which is interchangeable with "the day of the Lord." The rapture happens between the 6th and 7th seals, and after the great tribulation, but before the day of the Lord, which day is viewed as the start of God's wrath (charts #2, 6).

PRETERISM (Full) - A view that opposes Futurism and Historicism. In regard to eschatology, "full" Preterism is a belief that all prophecy has been fulfilled in the 1st century; most all before, or at 70 A.D. The view holds that the destruction of Jerusalem, the parousia of Christ, and the resurrection of the dead, are all past. The resurrection was not the raising of physical bodies, but rather a spiritual resurrection of the souls from Hades, who, if saved, obtained heavenly bodies. The wicked were cast into the lake of fire. Many Preterists believe the process of the resurrection and judgment is ongoing and will be until the end of history. II Peter 3 would be interpreted to be a description of the destruction of Jerusalem in 70 A.D. The "new heaven and new earth" is the spiritual kingdom that we are now in, thus replacing the "old heaven and old earth" which was the temple system. However, most Preterists reject universalism and Annihilationism. Many Preterists believe the harlot city in Revelation was the city of Jerusalem, thus the judgment against it. It is also taught that all of the "special" gifts ceased in 70 A.D.. "Partial" Preterism, which constitutes most types of Preterists, differs from "Full" Preterism, in the view of the resurrection and the advent. Partial Preterists see the coming of Christ in 70 A.D. as one for judgment only and not the rapture or resurrection of the saints, while Full Preterists believe that all events have taken place already. Both believe in a future resurrection at the end of history, but the Full Preterists hold to a "spiritual" return of Christ and a "spiritual" resurrection only, while the Partial Preterists believe in a future bodily return of Christ, with a bodily resurrection. The Full Preterism view of the resurrection, and the return of Christ would seem to violate all historical Christian creeds as well as scripture. Both will be either post-millennialists, or amillennialists.

RAPTURE - A non-biblical term, accepted by most positions, to identify the "rapturing up" or "catching away" of all living believers at the return of Christ. This rapture happens, simultaneously, with the resurrection of all deceased Christians from all ages. (I Thessalonians 4:14-17; II Thessalonians 2:1; Isaiah 26:19-21). All believers dead or alive will meet Jesus Christ in the air at His return and will be with Him forever (the dead are raised first). We could use the words, "translation of the saints," but the term rapture is ok too; it simply means to "snatch away." The timing (and not the fact of) of the rapture is perhaps the most controversial aspect of prophecy and, unfortunately, has caused much grief in Christian circles, much like the debate of John Wesley and George Whitfield on the preaching of predestination and election vs. free grace, which both debates will continue until we see Christ face to face (chart #2).

RESTRAINER, THE - This is title given to an unidentified personage. The pre-tribbers believe it to be the Holy Spirit so as to support their theory that the Church is removed at the start of the week. Some believe that it is Michael the archangel (Rosenthal and authors belief), and still others have varying opinions to include the Pope, civil government, Nero, etc. The Bible simply is not clear as to his identity.

RESURRECTION OF BELIEVERS - The time when Christ will raise the bodies of all believers from their graves and reunite them with their deceased souls that He brings from Heaven. This happens in an instantaneous moment in time when believers will be changed from the mortal to the immortal and will live eternally with Christ (I Corinthians 15:51-53; I Thessalonians 3:13; Jude 14; Isaiah 26:19). There are however, great differences of opinion as to when this happens and the nature of the body when it is raised. The pre-trib camp view the Church (saints) being raised at the start of the week, having immortal bodies, and then 7 years later, see the martyred believers (saints) being raised in mortal bodies along with the surviving saints. These saints will reproduce and bear children who rebel against Christ at the end of the 1000 years. The post-tribbers see the Church (saints) and all believers from the New and Old Testaments being raised at once and receiving their immortal bodies to rule and reign with Christ in His kingdom. The ones who convert and follow the ways of Christ during the millennium will reside in mortal bodies.

REVEALING OF ANTICHRIST - A time when Antichrist's identity is uncovered to the Jews and to the rest of the world. The pre-trib belief is that he is revealed at the beginning of the week. All the rest of the positions see him as being revealed when he commits the abomination of desolation in the middle of the week, and also surrounds Jerusalem with his armies (Daniel 9:27; Luke 21:20).

SAINTS - A term used 95 times in the Bible; 34 times in the Old Testament, and 61 times in the New Testament. The saints are all believers and possess eternal life. The pre-trib believers do not agree that the "saints" in the book of Revelation (who gave their lives for the witness of Jesus) are a part of the Church and will not be raptured or have immortal bodies. The post-trib and pre-wrath believe that the saints are part of the Church and will be treated the same as all believers in Christ. Note: Careful thought and consideration should be given to the idea that the martyred tribulation saints are not part of the Church and will be treated differently with regard to sealing of the Holy Spirit, and affording them immortal bodies. There should be very specific scripture to back up such a thought.

THREE WOES, THE - The references to these are found in Revelation 9:12 and 11:14. They represent, and are interchangeable with, the 5th, 6th, and 7th trumpets. The third woe is the 7th trumpet and is the entire 7 vials (bowls) judgments. Pre-wrath and post-tribulationists both see the 7 vials as starting at the end of the week, while many pre-tribbers see the event occurring during the tribulation.

TIME OF REWARDS - A time for all believers to receive their rewards according to their works that were done with the right motive (II Cor. 5:10). This is commonly called the "bema seat" judgment in theological circles. Christ is the foundation and we are the builders of the "superstructure." If what we build on the foundation, while on earth, is worthless then our rewards will be in proportion. The time of this judgment and rewards will be at the appearing and kingdom of Christ (II Timothy 4:1, 8). However, most pre-trib adherents believe the rewards are given out while up in Heaven during the great tribulation.

TWO WITNESSES, THE - These are two unknown identities mentioned in Revelation, chapter 11. They are two beings that are given supernatural powers by God, for the purpose of prophesying for 3-1/2 years during the 70th week. They can withhold rain, control the waters by turning them into blood, and the can plague any part of the earth at will. When their mission is completed, they will be killed by the beast from the bottomless pit. Their bodies will lie in the streets of Jerusalem for 3-1/2 days, but then will be raised from the dead and caught up to Heaven in the clouds. The speculation of their identity is held to be: Moses, Elijah, Enoch, and angelic or angelic like beings. Some place their witnessing in the first half of the week (pre-tribbers), while others place it in the second half of the week (post-tribbers and most others).

WAR IN HEAVEN - This war in Heaven will be the time when Satan and his angels fight against Michael and his angels and Satan is defeated. He is cast out of Heaven permanently and is cast down to the earth to persecute the saints and the inhabitants of Israel. Before this, he had access to Heaven and accused the saints before God, day and night (Rev. 12:10). He will temporarily control the world through his angels and demons for approximately 3-1/2 years. It is mostly agreed by all positions that this happens in the middle of the 70th week when he empowers Antichrist to perform miracles to convince the world that Antichrist is God. The event coincides with the abomination of desolation. The text that is used is found in Revelation, chapter 12:7-17.

WHEAT AND THE TARES - This is a parable spoken by Jesus to the Jews and the Apostles about the kingdom of Heaven. It was a picture of how the saved and the unsaved would be dealt with at the end of the age. The parable told of a farmer who planted seed, but when it started to spring up he found the weeds mixed in with the good seed. He told his laborers to let them grow together until harvest time, at which time he would harvest the good crop and then burn all the weeds. After the multitude of Jews left, he interpreted the parable, and its meaning, privately to his disciples. The sower of the good seed was Christ, the farmers field was the world, the good seed was those who were saved, and the sower of the weeds was Satan. They were told that, at the end of the age, Christ would send forth His angels and separate the wicked from among the just. The wicked (tares) would be dealt with first, though the vials and Armageddon. The full text is taken from Matthew 13:24-30, 36-43, 49-50.

WRATH OF GOD - In future prophecy, it is a time when God pours out His "undiluted" wrath upon the people who are wicked and unrepentant. The "wrath of God" is a controversial term, and is interchangeable with the day of the Lord; it is much debated because it affects the location of the rapture. The pre-tribbers see it as starting at the beginning of the 70th week of Daniel, while the pre-wrath people view it as starting with the 7 trumpets (which is placed in the 2nd half of the week). The post-tribbers envision it starting with the 7 vials at the end of the week. All positions include the 7 vials and Armageddon in the wrath. The pre-wrath and author's post-trib positions both agree that the wrath of God is introduced at the 6th seal, and then the 7th seal, which is the 7 vials, is when the wrath actually begins. Both see the rapture as in-between the 6th and 7th seals.

1335TH DAY - We get this day from the book of Daniel, chapter 12:11. It is an extension of time past the close of the 70th week in the amount of 75 days, or 2-1/2 months. The mention of it, in context, would suggest that this is the "official" start of the 1000 year kingdom period, but it is not known for sure just what it represents. There are many events transpiring at the close of the week, which would include a complete restoration of the earth, judgments, burning of weaponry, burying of the dead, the giving of rewards, assignment of reigning positions, the building of the new temple, etc.

144,000 - This is a number given in chapters 7 and 14 of Revelation describing the 12 Jewish tribes who were to be sealed from the wrath of God's judgments. There are 12,000 from each tribe, with the tribe of Dan noticeably missing, having been replaced with Manasseh, one of Joseph's children. Not all agree on why Dan is missing, and not all agree that the 144,000 in chapter 14 are the same group. Some see these 144,000 as being the Church, while most view them as the same group of sealed Jews as in chapter 7.

7 SEALS OF JUDGMENT - These are judgments that God allows on the earth because of man's failure to obey Him. They appear to be carried out by humans as opposed to angels, with most agreeing that the first one starts at the beginning

of the week. The first four of the seals are often called the "four horses of the apocalypse," which affect about 1/4th of the earth or people. All rapture positions place the 6th seal in different locations in the week; they are placed: at the first half of the week (pre-trib), somewhere in the 2nd half (pre-wrath), and at the very end (post-trib - author).

7 TRUMPETS OF JUDGMENT - These judgments of God fall upon the earths inhabitants during the 70th week. There is a difference of opinion as to whether they are somewhat concurrent with the seals, or whether they are consecutive. It is believed by many that the 7th trumpet is the final trump before the return of Christ, believed to be at the end of the week. Others end the 7th trumpet in the middle of the week. Whenever they occur, these judgments are much more intense then the seal judgments, and are implimented by angels.

7 VIALS OF JUDGMENT - These are the final angelic judgments or plagues upon mankind before the return of Christ, and just before the battle of Armageddon. They are the most intense of the 21 judgments involving monumental worldwide devastation. Again, there is controversy as to when they start and when they are completed. All agree that they occur at the tail end of the week, or just on the outside. Pre-wrath and post-trib (author's model) place them immediately outside the close of the week, while pre-tribbers place them inside.

70TH WEEK OF DANIEL - This is a reference to a specific Jewish prophecy in the Old Testament given to Daniel by an angel during Judah's captivity in Babylon. The prophecy and covered a great expanse of time from 445 B.C. (most agreed upon date), to the time when Christ comes at a future time to the Mount of Olives in Jerusalem. The weeks represent years because of the Hebrew word "Sheva," or "Shabua," meaning seven. The 70 weeks are not continuous however, and there is a "pause" between the 69th and the 70th week, to which all pre-millennial futurist students of the Word agree. The prophecy was one that saw the future crucifixion of Christ, the captivity of Jerusalem in 70 A.D. and it foretold the final 7 years of mans history before Christ took back the title deed of the earth. The prophecy consisted of 70 weeks of years covering a total of 490 years, with the last 7 not yet fulfilled. If you are amillennial in your position, then you believe the prophecy has already been fulfilled in early Church history (chart #3).

About the Author

After 35 years of study, and now by the pressing of the Holy Spirit, Roy Anderberg has come to the point where he senses the need to take a stand on what he believes is a rational understanding of eschatology. He does not suggest that all debated questions can be dogmatically answered; yet some points he has been heavily burdened  with and feels the need to share his thoughts and views with others who also have an interest in future events. He is seeking only to do God's will, which is why it has taken so many years to see this book come to print. Roy is a God honoring father, and a husband of 47 years to a godly wife. He holds no fear of criticism nor rebuke, and believes the study of end time prophecy (eschatology) needs to be taught in the church, now, more then ever before. Time is not standing still, and every moment that passes by, brings us closer to the return of Christ and the end of time as we know it.

In keeping with the scriptures, Roy is holding his light high on top of the mountain for all to see and consider. We are instructed, by God, to study the Word that we may rightly divide the Word of truth. Read this book with the knowledge that it was not the product of some whimsical effort to fill your bookshelf with just another end times fictional story. This is a non-fiction book of biblical exegetical study with as much discernment as possible, and yet is easily understood by laymen.

Roy has followed his calling to study the issues and consider all the popular viewpoints of today; you now get the benefit of all those years of work. He champions his viewpoint yet does not browbeat the reader into compliancy. Each of the issues addressed is presented to the reader for the purpose of making up their own mind and to decide for themselves which one is most scripturally correct; not only in interpretation, but intent also.

CPSIA information can be obtained at www.ICGtesting.com
Printed in the USA
LVOW10s1353200713

343856LV00002B/585/P